Super
Spellers

STARTER
SETS

Super
Spellers

STARTER
SETS

Mark Weakland

Stenhouse
PUBLISHERS

www.stenhouse.com

Library of Congress Cataloging-in-Publication Data

Names: Weakland, Mark, author.
Title: Super spellers starter sets / Mark Weakland.
Description: Portsmouth, New Hampshire : Stenhouse Publishers, [2018] |
  Includes bibliographical references.
Identifiers: LCCN 2018034199 (print) | LCCN 2018052519 (ebook) | ISBN
  9781625312723 (ebook) | ISBN 9781625312716 (pbk. : alk. paper)
Subjects: LCSH: English language—Orthography and spelling—Study and
  teaching (Elementary) | English language—Composition and exercises—Study
  and teaching (Elementary) | Reading.
Classification: LCC LB1574 (ebook) | LCC LB1574 .W375 2018 (print) | DDC
  372.63/2—dc23

LC record available at https://lccn.loc.gov/2018034199

Cover design, interior design, and typesetting by Lucian Burg,
LU Design Studios, Portland, ME

Manufactured in the United States of America

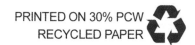

PRINTED ON 30% PCW
RECYCLED PAPER

25 24 23 22 21 20 19   9 8 7 6 5 4 3 2 1

DEDICATION

To dedicated and caring teachers everywhere

CONTENTS

ACKNOWLEDGMENTS

I wish to thank everyone at Stenhouse Publishing; editor Terry Thompson, who provided guidance, know-how, and kind support during the writing and shaping of this book; Meg Grossman, Stephanie Green, and Megan Marquez, who helped me troubleshoot the lesson sets; and all the researchers and writers, past and present, who have contributed to my ever-evolving understanding of literacy.

INTRODUCTION

Spelling is for reading. Spelling is also for writing. These two thoughts inform every aspect of this book. Teachers can help their students become better readers by providing spelling instruction that (1) teaches children to notice, manipulate, and remember patterns in words and (2) gives them opportunities to move word parts and whole words into their "brain's dictionary" via spelling activities, daily writing, and weekly spelling tests. Likewise, teachers can boost their students' writing fluency by teaching them specific spelling strategies (how to spell a word) and then giving them multiple chances to practice those strategies in all types of writing.

Noticing patterns, using strategies to spell unknown words, thinking about meaning, hearing sounds and then applying letters to spell, knowing how to spell versus knowing what to spell, practicing spelling through writing: These actions and ideas are thoroughly explored and discussed in my book *Super Spellers: Seven Steps to Transforming Your Spelling Instruction* (2017). They are present in this book, too, but here they take the form of lesson sets ready for use in your classroom. In upcoming chapters, you will find effective and easy-to-implement spelling centers, ways to teach spelling strategies (used by children to solve their spelling challenges), and methods for teaching everything from

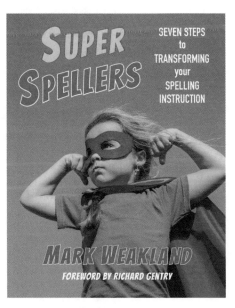

Super Spellers: Seven Steps to Transforming Your Spelling Instruction

short vowel patterns to multisyllabic Greek- and Latin-based words. Every one of these lesson sets is designed to help students notice and remember the spellings of patterns and words and to move those patterns and words into the lexicons in their brains.

This book uses the term *lesson sets* because you will present the spelling features of each "set" (such as the *ar* and *or* patterns or the prefixes *pre*, *re*, and *de*) over multiple days, in multiple lessons, and in multiple ways. Every lesson set gives you the materials, teaching guidance, and teaching language you need for a week's worth of instruction. But this book is *not* a spelling program, and therefore you will not see fully realized, day-to-day lessons. It will be up to you to introduce the spelling features as you see fit, choose and possibly adapt the word lists, and pick and choose from a menu of daily activities. At the end of it all, you will be able to use the knowledge you gain from this book to create lesson sets of your own.

What's in the Book?

Because spelling is for reading, it is important to teach spelling, not merely assign it. Fortunately, you have in your hands everything you need to begin efficient and effective spelling instruction. In Chapter 1 you will find lesson sets for teaching spelling strategies. Teach these sets to show your students how to use a strategy (or strategies) to spell an unknown word. Chapter 2 contains lesson sets for constructing spelling centers and then teaching children how to use them. And Chapters 3 and 4 hold almost two dozen lesson sets on specific spelling features, from CVC short vowel words and words that contain vowel teams to consonant-*le* words and words built on Greek and Latin roots.

These lesson sets are not based on a scope and sequence from any particular spelling program. But each set focuses on a spelling feature typically taught within the associated grade band. Thus, in Grade Band 1–3 you will find a lesson set for teaching the vowel-consonant-*e* pattern, typically taught in first grade. Meanwhile, in Grade Band 3–5 you will find lessons on prefixes and suffixes, which are often taught in third or fourth grade. Regardless of its particular spelling feature or grade band, each lesson set contains the same components:

- A focus for the week (or instructional cycle)
- Options for skill review and reteaching
- A master spelling list of words for word study activities and differentiated word lists
- A pre-test that helps you determine what students know so you can create differentiated groups
- At least two examples of differentiated word lists

- Look Touch Say language for presenting a quick and easy spelling activity while giving your students practice in multiple strategies, day to day and throughout the week

- A blackline master of word cards for word-sorting activities that help students explore patterns, see relationships between words, and construct meaning

- Word ladders that teach children to notice sounds and letters, explore patterns within words, and learn the meaning of word parts and whole words

- Suggestions for language to use during word and sentence dictation activities

Please remember that this book's lesson sets are only a start. They do not constitute a complete curriculum. Therefore, one of this book's goals is to help you internalize the lesson components to the point that you can create additional lesson sets for any spelling feature or convention you want to teach. Through repeated practice and reflective teaching, the routines will become habit and the ideas that underlie the instruction will become deeply known. If, however, you want to more fully explore the ideas, strategies, and activities spelled out in this book, consider picking up a copy of *Super Spellers*.

Connecting Stand-Alone Lessons to Reading and Writing

We know that effective spelling instruction not only activates reading circuitry but also creates the neural pathways and cognitive "wiring" that lead to higher reading achievement (Seidenberg 2016; McCandliss, Wise, and Yoncheva 2015; Rapp and Lipka 2011). As the orthographic area of the brain gains in importance, encoding and decoding develop. Soon patterns of all types are recognized and stored by the brain. Eventually words are saved in their entirety, ready for later use in reading and writing. Student brains, and adult brains, too, activate this repository of words and draw upon it during fluent reading and writing.

Stand-alone spelling lessons, like the ones you are about to encounter, are a critical part of reading instruction. But other types of instruction play a role, too. I encourage you to directly, explicitly, and repeatedly make connections between the spelling of words and the reading and writing of them. Here are a few easy ways to connect spelling to reading and writing:

1. Do a word hunt. Start with text that has been previously read. For example, ask your students to choose a favorite book, story, or article they've read this week. Then send them on a word hunt, where they find words that match the spelling features of the week (or from previous lessons). A word hunt can be done as an ending activity in a guided reading group, as a whole-group activity after a shared story, or as a word study center.

2.   Have students read. The more children read, the greater chance they have of improving their fluency, building their background knowledge, and increasing their vocabulary. When kids read greater amounts of text, they increase their chances of committing whole words to their brain dictionaries, thus becoming better spellers, too.

3.   Have students write. Writing widely, like reading widely, exposes students to more words and adds to their background knowledge of how words are spelled. When children write, they think about spelling. They see words over and over again as they revise and read their writing and as they share it with multiple audiences (a buddy, the classroom, a parent). So, the question becomes "How can you program more writing opportunities into your teaching day, especially ones that are authentic, engaging, and enjoyable?" I suggest you consider writing workshop. Process-based, authentic writing increases the chances that your students will see writing as a meaningful and enjoyable activity. When kids enjoy writing and see it as a meaningful thing to do, they are much more likely to *want* to write. Eagerness to write leads to more writing, which leads to greater writing ability in general. More immediately, it gives students opportunities to practice spelling based on sound, pattern, and meaning, as well as to put scores of words into their brain dictionaries.

Spelling Instruction: How Often and for How Long?

Spelling should be directly and explicitly linked to reading (including vocabulary) and writing (including grammar). But spelling instruction needs to be much more than a reference to letters and patterns during reading time and a chunk of instruction during writing time. Spelling instruction needs to take place daily for a dedicated amount of time. It also needs to incorporate engaging and effective spelling activities, a variety of words focused on just a few concepts, and a weekly spelling list.

During dedicated spelling time, word study occurs, patterns are explored, and strategies are explained, modeled, and practiced. This instruction leads to not only higher spelling and writing achievement but higher reading achievement, too. This is because best-practice spelling instruction strengthens brain areas involved in orthographic processing. The brain's orthographic processing system stores the correct spellings of thousands of words. This robust lexicon of words (or "mind dictionary") is critical to fluent reading, regardless of whether you are a child or adult.

How much time should you devote to spelling instruction? Approximately fifteen to twenty minutes a day will serve your students well. If your students are struggling to read, write, and spell, you may want to provide more time. This instruction will be in service to reading and writing, so don't think of it as time you have to "give up" to do spelling. Think of it as time devoted to teaching skills that lead to more fluent reading and writing, especially for those students who struggle.

Here is one possible outline for a five-day cycle of spelling instruction:

Day 1: Twenty Minutes

- Pre-test (six–seven minutes).

- Introduction to spelling features of the week (thirteen–fourteen minutes). This time is for direct and explicit instruction on sounds and letters, patterns, meaning parts of words, or spelling conventions. Introduce words and concepts to the whole group, model what you want students to do, and engage in think-alouds.

Day 2: Fifteen Minutes

- Review your spelling feature focus.

- Do a Look Touch Say introductory activity. (Activities are introduced one at a time, over time. Early in the year, model how to do the activity, and then guide your students as they practice.) Use your pre-test data, which you will have previously analyzed, to help you differentiate instruction and content.

Day 3: Fifteen–Twenty Minutes

- Reteach sounds, letters, patterns, or conventions with direct and explicit instruction as necessary.

- Through spelling activities, give students the opportunity to practice their spelling strategies and move word patterns and whole words into their brains' lexicons. Choose from any of the following activities:
  - Look Touch Say activity
  - Spelling grids using manipulatives, paper and pencil, or electronic tablet
  - Word dictation
  - Word sorts
  - Word ladders
  - Opportunity to go to a spelling or word study center

Day 4: Fifteen–Twenty Minutes

- Choose from any of the following activities:
    - Look Touch Say
    - Spelling grids
    - Word or sentence dictation
    - Flip folders
    - Word ladders
    - Practice tests with instant error correction
    - Opportunity to go to a spelling or word study center

Day 5: Ten Minutes

- Weekly quiz with instant error correction.

Every elementary school teacher knows that it's a challenge to get through an instructional day with no interruptions. There are assemblies; fire and safety drills; school pictures; holiday parties; disruptions caused by barfing, bleeding, and misbehaving; and _____ (fill in the blank). The list is endless.

If one day of your instructional cycle is interrupted and you need to make up time by cutting spelling, consider axing Day 4 of the schedule. But if your week is greatly disrupted and you feel the need to cut two days of spelling instruction to make up time, consider teaching one lesson set over two weeks. This is much better than rushing through one lesson set in three days (which leads to "memorize and move on" teaching). Additional days of spelling instruction give students time to deeply study patterns and meaning. That's a good thing! And if you have on hand a master word list that is narrow and rich (meaning that it focuses on only two to four spelling features but contains thirty to forty words), you will have more than enough words to use for activities that take place over six or seven days of instruction that occurs over a two-week span.

Here's a possible schedule for a seven-day cycle of instruction.

Day 1: Twenty Minutes

- Pre-test (six–seven minutes).
- Introduction to spelling features of the week (thirteen–fourteen minutes). This time is for direct and explicit instruction on sounds

and letters, patterns, meaning parts of words, or spelling conventions. Introduce words and concepts to the whole group, model what you want students to do, and engage in think-alouds.

Day 2: Fifteen Minutes

- Review your spelling feature focus.
- Do a Look Touch Say introductory activity. (Activities are introduced one at a time, over time. Early in the year, model how to do the activity, and then guide your students as they practice.) Use your pre-test data to help you begin to differentiate instruction and content.

Day 3: Fifteen–Twenty Minutes

- Reteach with direct and explicit instruction if necessary.
- Choose from any of the following:
  - Look Touch Say activity
  - Spelling grids using manipulatives, paper and pencil, or electronic tablet
  - Word dictation
  - Word sorts
  - Word ladders
  - Opportunity to go to a spelling or word study center

Day 4: Fifteen–Twenty Minutes

- Reteach with direct and explicit instruction if necessary.
- Choose from any of the following:
  - Look Touch Say
  - Spelling grids
  - Word or sentence dictation
  - Flip folders
  - Practice test with instant error correction
  - Opportunity to go to a spelling or word study center

Day 5: Ten Minutes

- Shared word hunt: Using a shared-reading text, students look for words built upon currently and previously studied spelling patterns. Class discusses word pronunciation and meaning.

Day 6: Ten Minutes

- Quiz with instant error correction.

Day 7: Fifteen–Twenty Minutes

- Have students write on a self-selected topic while focusing on how to spell words correctly, both during writing and after writing. Guide them in the use of spelling strategies, including the "Circle, Come Back, Correct" strategy. (See next chapter for a description.)

This introduction gives you suggested spelling schedules and ideas for connecting stand-alone spelling instruction to daily reading and writing, as well as a broad overview of the centers, strategies, and lessons found within this book. Now it's time to dig in and decide where you want to start.

I suggest you first flip through the pages and scan the materials. Let everything percolate for a bit. Compare what you see in the chapters with your current content and instruction. Then pick a starting point. Perhaps you will start slowly, introducing your class to a flip folder center or a Look Touch Say routine with your current word lists. Maybe you will pick a slightly more ambitious path and plan a series of monthly lessons (and an anchor chart to go with them) that introduce your students to the half-dozen strategies spellers use to spell unknown words. Or maybe you'll want to dive in and map out a semester's worth of spelling lessons, using lesson sets in this book as well as lessons you create, based on what you learn here.

No matter where you start or how quickly you progress, know that by making a commitment to transforming your spelling instruction, you are making a commitment to your students. Keep taking steps to learn why spelling is for reading (as well as for writing), and keep working to implement spelling instruction that is rooted in best practice. You'll be pleased with the results. More students in your classroom will be engaged and capable spellers. Your struggling students will stand a better chance of becoming fluent, capable readers and writers. And you will gain a sense of success and satisfaction, knowing you have taken your instruction to a new, higher level.

CHAPTER 1

Lesson Sets for Teaching Spelling Strategies

Introduction to Spelling Strategies

Students use spelling strategies to spell words on their spelling tests. More importantly, they use strategies to write the words they want to see in their narrative, informational, and opinion writing. The expectation is for students to use spelling strategies automatically and independently while writing. But it takes some work to get the majority of kids in a classroom to that point. After explicitly teaching and modeling strategies, you will need to give your students encouragement and time to practice them during guided and independent writing. I would be a rich man if I'd gotten a dime every time a student asked me, "Mr. Weakland, how do you spell _____?" And I would be a poor man if I had given up a quarter every time I answered, "Don't ask me that question. Use a strategy."

Before you teach spelling strategies and have students practice them, it's best to raise your students' awareness about the general state of their spelling. One way to do this is to tell them, "Even professional writers make spelling mistakes." Follow that with "All writers work to fix their spelling mistakes." What you are telling students is that it's okay to spell a word incorrectly while writing, but it is *not* okay to fail to go back and fix spelling mistakes.

Once your students know they will make errors and you expect them to fix them, model how *you* make mistakes while spelling and then take action to correct them. In the end, you want students to know that when writers don't know how to spell a word, they purposefully employ a strategy. Every writer should have the goal of becoming a self-aware, self-monitoring, self-correcting spelling checker.

In my mind, there are six basic spelling strategies to teach:

1. Hear and spell the sounds.

2. Spell by analogy (use a word you know).

3. See the word in your head.

4. Think about meaning.

5. Use a mnemonic (make a memory aid).

6. Circle, come back, correct.

Spelling Strategies

The first four strategies are intimately tied to reading, specifically the various ways that readers read words. The fifth is a little "trick" kids can use to help them remember how to spell an especially difficult word. The sixth is a spelling strategy for writing.

The remainder of this chapter presents lesson sets for teaching these six strategies. In Appendix A, you'll find a blackline master you can copy and put up as a poster in your classroom. For a more personalized option, use the poster as a guide for developing a self-made anchor chart. Anchor charts give you the opportunity to use the language that is most appropriate for your students.

Regardless of whether you use a copied poster or classroom-created anchor chart, remember to introduce and practice the strategies cumulatively. First, figure out which strategy your students need most. Then teach that strategy using think-alouds and modeling. Finally, give kids time to practice the strategies. When and where does this practice occur? It occurs daily and weekly during spelling activities, work study centers, and spelling tests, and every time students engage in writing.

Once the majority of your students have mastered one strategy, move on to another one. Use formative assessment to determine which strategy the majority of the class needs the most. How do you decide if students are using a strategy to the point of mastery? One easy way is to monitor them as they write and spell and then ask them directly (during an activity, writing time, or practice test), "How are

Spelling Strategy Classroom Survey Sheets

you spelling that word?" "Why did you spell it that way?" and "What strategy did you use to spell that word?" If, after listening to their answers, you believe your students would benefit from using a different strategy, teach them the one they need the most. You may want to use a simple checklist to help you keep track of who is using what strategy and when they are using it. Appendix C contains two assessment sheets you can use to track strategy usage.

Here's an example of one assessment:

Date_____

"How did you spell that word?"

"What strategy did you use?"

"Why did you spell it that way?"

Student	Strategy				
	Sounds/Letters	Analogy	Sight	Mnemonic	Meaning
Raymond	✔	✔	✔		
Clarice					
Destiny			✔		
Hunter B.					
Juelz	✔			✔	
Katie					
Ty					

Regarding the teaching of spelling strategies, here's something else to consider. Spelling strategies are taught through dedicated lessons. You should, however, mention, review, and reteach strategies even as you teach lessons on spelling features. For example, during a lesson cycle in which you are teaching the *oi/oy* vowel teams, you can remind children that they can spell *spoil* by segmenting the sounds and then assigning letters to each sound, thinking of a word they know (such as *foil*) and using it to spell another word (such as *spoil*), working to "see" *spoil* in their heads every time they write it, and so on. The language you use during your spelling instruction should reflect an emphasis on strategies. Thus, every week and during most lessons, consider using language such as this:

- "Spellers use strategies to help them spell words."

- "What strategies have we learned so far? Let's review them."

- "What strategy might we use to spell this word?"

- "Let's review and practice using our 'make a memory aid' strategy. We haven't talked about that one all month."

Teaching "Hear and Spell the Sounds"

Overview

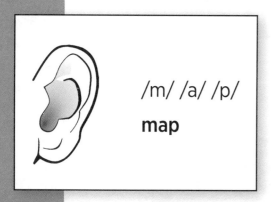

Hear and spell sounds

In the earliest stages of spelling, children hear the sounds of a word (aloud or in their heads) and then encode those sounds into letters. The six lessons of this lesson set help students learn to do those things. The first three build phonemic awareness—i.e., the awareness that words are made up of sounds. In Lesson D, letters are attached to the sounds. Lesson F focuses on how to get children to accurately count the number of syllables in a word.

You may not need to teach every lesson on this strategy. Lessons can be combined or excluded. Conversely, you may need to reteach a lesson (multiple times) if your students are not using the strategy correctly or at all.

Lesson A: Stretch the Word to Hear the Sounds

When first teaching this strategy, use CVC, CCVC, or CVCC words, especially ones containing letters that can be "held out," such as the vowels, the consonants *f, l, m, n, s, v,* and *z,* and the digraphs *sh* and *th (voiced and unvoiced).* Here is a list of words that work well for this lesson:

fat	that
let	lip
mop	snip
flap	not
slap	thin
shop	this
lump	send

Begin by teaching your students how to "stretch the word." Tell them a word is like a big rubber band. Model how to say the word, grab hold of either end of it (make two fists and hold them in front of you), and then slowly stretch it by pulling your hands away from each other as you say the word's sounds, holding out the vocalization of each phoneme. For example, *let* becomes lllll-eeeeeeee-t, *map* becomes mmm-aaaa-p, and *flop* becomes fffff-llllllll-oooo-p.

Lesson B: Stretch and Zap the Sounds in a Word

For this lesson, use the words from Lesson A. This time, after you stretch and say a word, zap out the sounds of the word.

To model zapping, make a fist. Next, segment the sounds by saying each one separately, pumping your hand and throwing out a finger for each one as you say it. For example, the word *it* gets two pumps. The index finger comes out when you say /i/. The middle finger comes out when you say /t/. Finally, draw your fingers back into a fist, blending the sounds together, and saying the word. "It."

The word *slip* gets four pumps. The index finger comes out when you say /s/. The middle finger comes out when you say /l/. Next comes the ring finger for /i/. Finally, the pinky comes out for /p/. End the zapping by drawing all four fingers back into a fist and saying "Slip."

Here is some language you could use to teach kids how to zap.

> **Teacher:** We know how to grab a word and stretch it to hear its sounds. Today I will teach you another way to hear the sounds of a word. It's called zapping. Watch me as I zap out the word *fish. Fish.* [Teacher says the word and makes a fist.] /f/ /i/ /sh/ [Teacher pumps hand, putting out a finger for each phoneme.] *Fish.* [Teacher pulls fingers back into a fist.] Watch: I'll do it one more time. [Teacher repeats the process.] Now you zap out sounds in *fish* with me. [Teacher and students zap out the word.]

To combine stretching and zapping, I suggest this language, which gives the outline of a small routine you can repeat daily.

Teacher: Our first word is *slap*. What's the word, everyone?

Students: *Slap.*

Teacher: Let's stretch *slap*.

Students and teacher*: [Everyone grabs the word with their fists and then pulls their fists apart as they say the word.] Sssss-llllll-aaaaa-p.*

Teacher: Let's zap the word *slap*. *Slap*. [Teacher says the word and makes a fist.] /s/ /l/ /a/ /p/. [Teacher pumps hand, putting out a finger for each phoneme.] *Slap*. [Teacher pulls fingers back into a fist.]

Teacher: The next word is *fish*. What's the word, everyone?

Students: *Fish.*

Teacher: Stretch it.

Students and teacher*: Fffff-iiiii-ssshhh.*

Teacher: Zap it! /F/ /i/ /sh/. [Teacher pumps hand, putting out a finger for each phoneme.] *Fish*. [Teacher pulls fingers back into a fist.]

Teacher: The next word is . . .

Lesson C: Zap the Sounds in a Word

When your students become skilled at hearing the individual sounds in a word, they no longer need to stretch it out to hear its sounds. This lesson goes right to zapping a word, which is more time efficient than stretching plus zapping. When giving words, it is important to say the word clearly and then have your students repeat it. Having students repeat the word before zapping gives you a chance to hear whether they are pronouncing it correctly. After all, a sound-letter speller can't spell an unknown word correctly if it isn't pronounced correctly.

Here are some words you can use:

set	thin
chip	got
slap	brush
flash	nod
fun	step
fib	cash
fresh	chin

And here is language outlining a routine that can be used as often as you want:

Teacher: Watch me as I zap out the word *chop. Chop.* [Teacher says the word and makes a fist.] /ch/ /o/ /p/. [Teacher pumps hand, putting out a finger for each phoneme.] *Chop.* [Teacher pulls fingers back into a fist.] Zap *chop* with me. [Teacher repeats and students zap out the word.]

Teacher: The next word is *ship.* What's the word, everyone?

Students: *Ship.*

Teacher: Zap the word with me. *Ship.* [Teacher says the word and makes a fist.] /sh/ /i/ /p/. [Teacher pumps hand, putting out a finger for each phoneme.] *Ship.* [Teacher pulls fingers back into a fist.]

Lesson D: Zap the Sounds and Then Spell the Sounds with Letters

Thus far, Lessons A, B, and C have concentrated on developing the ability to phonemically segment a word. Up to this point, no letters have been attached to the sounds, and no actual spelling with letters has occurred.

Once your students understand zapping and can quickly and accurately phonemically segment a word such as *flash*, it's time to introduce spelling with letters. In an early stage of spelling development, spelling involves associating one letter with one sound. Later, combinations of letters are used to represent one sound (such as *ck* for /k/ and *eigh* for /ay/).

Elkonin boxes or spelling grids help students see that words are made of sounds (represented by boxes in the grid) and that each sound in a box has a letter or letters associated with it. The following dialogue gives you an idea of how to combine zapping the sounds of a word and spelling those sounds with letters in a spelling grid.

Teacher: In this lesson, we are going to zap words and then spell the sounds using the spelling grid on our whiteboards. We will use the strategy "Hear and Spell the Sounds." What strategy will we use, everyone?

Students: "Hear and Spell the Sounds."

Teacher: Watch me. Our first word is *chop. Chop.* [Teacher says the word and makes a fist.] /ch/ /o/ /p/. [Teacher pumps hand, putting out a finger for each phoneme.] *Chop.* Now I am going to write a letter or a digraph for each sound. Each spelling part goes in one box. The first sound is /ch/. /ch/ is spelled *c-h*, so I am going to write a *c* and an *h* in the first box. That's the digraph *ch.* [Teacher writes *ch* in first box of spelling grid.] The next sound is /o/. /o/ is spelled *o*. So, I write *o* in the second box. [Teacher writes *o* in second box of spelling grid.] Now I have /ch/ /o/. The last sound is /p/. I know that /p/ is spelled *p*, so I write a *p* in the last box. Now I have /ch/ /o/ /p/, *chop*!

ch		

ch	o	

ch	o	p

Teacher: [Teacher points to each box, reads each sound, and then runs pointer finger under all the boxes to read the word *chop*.] I'm going to erase my word. Now let's all zap the word *chop* and write it in our own spelling grids. What's the word, everyone?

Students: *Chop.*

Teacher: Zap it. *Chop.* [Teacher says the word and makes a fist.] /ch/ /o/ /p/. [Teacher pumps hand, putting out a finger for each phoneme.] *Chop.* [Teacher pulls fingers back into a fist.]

Teacher: Take your marker caps off. Spell *chop* on your spelling grid. Then put your caps back on. [Students spell. Teacher monitors.]

Teacher: Let's hear and spell another word. The word is *fish.* What's the word, everyone?

Students: *Fish.*

Teacher: Zap it with me. /f/ /i/ /sh/. [Teacher and students pump hands, putting out a finger for each phoneme.] *Fish.* [Teacher pulls fingers back into a fist.]

Teacher: Take your marker caps off. Spell *fish* on your spelling grid. Then put your caps back on.

f		

f	i	

f	i	sh

In Appendix B, you will find two spelling grid blackline masters. The first presents a series of grids of increasing length. This page allows students to find and use a grid with the exact number of squares for the exact number of sounds in the target word. For example, students would spell the word *fish* using the grid with three squares, but for the word *shrimp,* they would use the grid with five squares. The second blackline master, however, has only one spelling grid, six boxes long and presented horizontally on the page. Because most monosyllabic words contain no more than five or six phonemes, this one grid can be used to spell words such as *fish, lips, shrimp,* and *prints.* For any word that contains fewer than six phonemes, one or more boxes will be left over.

To create a set of spelling grids for your class, decide which master you want to use and make enough copies for every child in your class. I like to print on card stock because I don't like my sheets to get "curly" when I laminate them. But paper is fine, too! Regardless of its material, laminate each copy. Now your students can print on them with dry erase markers.

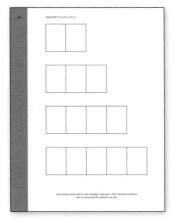 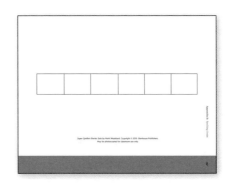

Spelling Grids

Lesson E: Zapping and Spelling Longer Words

Once students become fluent with zapping and associating the sounds with letters, move to words with more sounds in each word. Ratchet up the complexity of your practice words from simple CVC words such as *nap* and *sit* to CCVCC words such as *stomp* and *brick*. If you think it is helpful for your students to continue using spelling grids, continue to use them. You can also differentiate, having most students zap and spell without grids but having those who need more support use them.

> **Teacher:** [Models zapping and spelling of *brick*.] First, I spell each sound of my word with a letter or a group of letters. [Teacher writes letters while saying the sounds.] Now I go back and check my spelling by reading the word. *Brick.*
>
> **Teacher:** Now you try it. Your first word is *stomp*. Say it.
>
> **Students:** *Stomp*. [They make a fist.]
>
> **Teacher:** Zap it.
>
> **Students:** /s/ /t/ /o/ /m/ /p/. [They pump their hands and throw out a finger for each sound, ending with all five fingers out. Then they draw their fingers back into a fist and say the word again.] *Stomp.*
>
> **Teacher:** Write it. [Teacher pauses while students write the word.]
>
> **Teacher:** Check your answer. The word *stomp* is spelled *s-t-o-m-p*. Correct your answer if you need to. If your word is correct and you want to put a star next to it, do so. [Students check, correct, and make a star.]
>
> **Teacher:** Our next word is *smash*. [Teacher repeats routine.]

Here are some examples of more complex words you might use in a lesson like this:

stomp	slash
flash	fresh
flips	sleds
drops	shrimp
stump	stamp
smash	slump
lump	send

Lesson F: Feel Your Chin Drop

By placing their hand under their chin, saying a target word softly and slowly, and counting the number of times their hand moves (i.e., the number of times their chin drops), students can easily break words into syllables. Next, they can zap and spell the sounds in each syllable cumulatively to spell a multisyllabic word.

To model the chin drop, place the tips of your fingers, with your hand palm down, firmly against the edge of your chin. Say the target word slowly but naturally. Start with long vowel words that cause a deep drop in your chin, such as *time* and *stone*. You can also say word parts or "nonsense" words, such as *ipe*, *afe*, and *obe*.

Feel your chin drop

Tell your students how many times your hand moved and why it moved: Every syllable has a vowel, and vowels make our chins move downward when we say them. Sometimes the movement is large and sometimes it's small. By the way, I greatly prefer using the chin drop, rather than the hand clap, to teach syllables. Mouths and chins move naturally and unerringly with syllables. Claps do not.

Next, model saying a word this way and have your students mirror what you are doing. Once you have practiced one-syllable words, move on to two-syllable words. To reinforce the idea that the number of chin drops equals the number of syllables, have your students count the number of times your chin and hand move downward as you say a multisyllabic word. Choose your words carefully. Words with long-*i* and long-*o* sounds are good places to start: *grapevine, railroad, silent, raincoat, highway, pilot*, and so on. Have your students repeat the words with you. Next say three-syllable words: *volcano, potato,*

October. Finally, mix up the words. After each pronunciation, ask your students how many syllables they felt. Ask older children or children more phonemically advanced to identify the second syllable in a three-syllable word, or the first. All of this draws attention to the sounds in words at the syllable level.

In subsequent lessons, combine the chin drop with zapping and spelling. In other words, say a word such as *catfish*, break it apart by syllables, zap the sounds and spell the sounds in the first syllable, and finally, zap the sounds and spell the sounds in the second syllable. Make sure you model how to keep the syllables in proximity to one another as you spell. There should be no space between the syllables or between the words in a compound word.

The following words are two-syllable, closed-syllable words. They are appropriate for an introductory lesson on multisyllabic words. Each syllable in each word follows the VC, CVC, CCVC, or CVCC pattern.

catfish	zigzag
hotshot	sunset
unclip	inside
upset	tomcat
dishpan	sunfish
bathtub	cobweb

Teaching "Spell by Analogy (Use a Word You Know)"

Overview

As spelling ability develops, children move from matching sounds with basic letters and letter combinations to hearing "chunks" of sounds in words (such as *ing*, *unk*, *irst*, and so on) and matching those chunks with spelling patterns. They can then use the patterns (or chunks) they know to spell unknown words that probably have the same chunks. Thus, children can use their knowledge of how to spell *first* to spell the word *thirst* or get close to the correct spelling of *worst*.

Use a word you know

As before, this strategy can be taught and retaught in a variety of ways. Here is a way to teach the strategy in two parts, hearing chunks and using patterns. (Note that spellers need to master the former before they can use the latter effectively.)

Lesson A: Hear the Chunk

When you first teach this strategy, use easy-to-hear single-syllable words such as *fat, sat, mop, flop, kid, skid,* and so on. Other appropriate words are vowel-consonant-*e* syllable words (such as *lake, strike,* and *smoke*), *r*-controlled syllable words (*corn, hard,* and *shirt*), and various vowel-team syllable words (*low, paid,* and *feet*).

Model for students how single-syllable words can be broken into two parts: onset and rime. The onset of a word is the beginning consonant sound or sounds before the vowel. The rime is the part of the word that includes the vowel and everything after it. Here's a chart that gives the onset and rime of some of the words I just mentioned. The chart also shows how the rime (pattern) from one word can be used to spell other words. Thus, if the first word is known, and if children can pick off the onset of the word, retain the rime, and add a new onset, they can spell a new unknown word using an old known word. This is the essence of spelling by analogy.

Word	Onset	Rime	Other Words That Use the Rime
fat	*f*	*at*	sat, mat, that
flop	*fl*	*op*	slop, crop, hop
smoke	*sm*	*oke*	woke, poke, joke
corn	*c*	*orn*	born, horn, shorn
low	*l*	*ow*	row, grow, slow

Begin by modeling how you break a word into onset and rime. With your back to your students (and your head turned over your shoulder, if you have a class that needs watching!), hold your hands next to each other and over your head, with your palms away from yourself. Say a word on your word list, such as *fat*. Then say *f* and *at*. As you say the onset, /f/, move your left hand away from your right. Then say *at*. As you say the rime, move your right hand farther from your left. Say the onset and rime once more: *f, at*. Emphasize the sounds with a hand movement. Then bring your hands back together and say the word *fat*.

Model a few other words and then have the kids practice with you. Here is some suggested language:

> **Teacher:** Watch me as I break this word into its beginning sound and its end pattern. *Fish.* /f/. [Say the sound, move your left hand away.] /ish/. [Say the sound, move your right hand away.] *Fish.* [Pull your hands back together, side by side.] Watch: I'll do it one more time. [Repeat the

process.] Now you hold up your hand and break apart *fish* with me. [You and the students break the word into onset and rime.]

Teacher: Our first word is *match*. What's the word, everyone?

Students: *Match.*

Teacher: Break it apart.

Students and teacher: /m/. [Say the sound and move left hand.] / atch/. [Say the sound and move right hand.] *Match.* [Move hands back together.]

Teacher: Our next word is *slap*. What's the word, everyone?

Students: *Slap.*

Teacher: Let's break *slap* into its beginning sounds and its end pattern.

Students and teacher: /sl/. [Say and move left hand.] /ap/. [Say and move right hand.] *Slap.* [Move hands back together.]

Teacher: Let's put the word back together. *Slap.* [Pull hands back, side by side.]

Lesson B: Using End Patterns to Spell a New Word

Now it is time to use the rime of a known word to spell an unknown word. Once again, model for students how single-syllable words can be broken into onset and rime. As before, turn and hold your hands over your head with your palms away, hands next to each other. Say a word on your word list, such as *card*. Then say *c* and *ard*. As you say the onset, move your left hand away from your right. As you say the rime, move your right hand farther from your left. Then bring your hands back together and say the word *card*.

Repeat the process, but this time, spell the onset and the rime as you sound them out. Make sure you say to your students, "When I spell the word, I make sure I put the end chunk right next to the beginning sounds. It's all one word, and I want to make sure it looks like one word."

Repeat the entire process with a new word that uses the same rime. Here is some language you could use:

Teacher: Watch me as I break this word into its beginning sound and its end pattern. *Dirt.* /d/ [Say sound, move left hand.] /irt/. [Say chunk, move right hand.] *Dirt.* [Pull your hands back together, side by side.] I'll do it one more time, but this time, I'll spell the beginning sound and the end pattern. [Model saying /d/ and writing *d*, saying /irt/ and writing *irt*.]

Teacher: A new word is *shirt*. What's the word, everyone?

Students: *Shirt*.

Teacher: If you can spell *dirt*, you can spell *shirt*. Let's break *shirt* into its beginning sound and its end pattern, and let's spell each part.

Students and teacher: /sh/. [Say sound, move left, write *sh*.] /irt/. [Say chunk, move right hand, write *irt*.] *Shirt*. [Run finger under word as you read it.]

Teacher: Running our finger under the letters and noticing the letters and patterns helps us cross-check our sounds and our letters. Do we have letters and patterns that match the sounds? Yes, we do!

Teaching "See the Word in Your Head"

Overview

See the word in your head

Ask an adult to spell a commonly misspelled word such as *guarantee* or *cemetery* and watch her behavior. Often, she will pause, spell the word out loud, write it down on paper, and then check to see if it "looks right." This speller is using the "See the Word in Your Head" spelling strategy, one that accomplished spellers often use. In this example, the speller is accessing her brain's orthographic processing system to draw down a word from her "brain dictionary." She sees the stored word in her mind's eye, writes it down, and then accesses it once more to make sure that what she has written matches what she has stored in her brain.

The "See the Word in Your Head" strategy can be, and should be, modeled and practiced. Here are some ideas for teaching it.

Teaching

As with all student-used strategies, begin by modeling how you conjure up the sight (inside your head) of the word you want to spell. Begin with basic words, such as *bike* for children in early stages of spelling development and *nature* for children in later stages. Here's an idea of the language you can use as you write and think out loud. The example word is *guarantee*, a word I often misspell.

Teacher: I am going to model how I use the "See the Word in Your Head" strategy to spell a word. Let's say I want to spell the word *guarantee*, as in, "I *guarantee* the movie is amazing."

The first thing I do is say the word. "*Guarantee*." As I say the word, I'm going to think about how to spell it. Saying a word softly often helps me see letters in my head.

Now, I'm going to write the word. I'm not positive about the first syllable, but still, I will write the word as best I can. [Teacher writes *gaurantee*.]

I'm pretty sure there's a *u* in the first syllable of this word, but I'm not exactly sure where the *u* goes. Now, when I look at the word I just spelled, it doesn't look quite right to me. So, I'm going to switch the position of the *a* and the *u* and spell it a second way. And I'm going to leave the first spelling there. [Teacher spells *guarantee* next to *gaurantee*.]

When I look at the two spellings, I think the second spelling "looks right." I think that is how the word is spelled. To check and make sure I have spelled it correctly, I'm going to look up this spelling in the dictionary. If it's in there, I know it is correct! Or I can check its spelling by typing the word into a Word document and doing a spelling check or entering it into a search engine. Using any of these methods, I can be sure that I've spelled the word correctly.

After you have modeled your thinking, have your students practice the strategy with words they have spelled in the past. Here are steps to follow:

1.   Ask them to spell a word such as *height*.

2.   Before they begin to write, tell them to close their eyes and try to see the word as they say it softly.

3.   Next, have them spell the word and look at it. Ask them to decide if the word "looks right."

4.   Finally, have them type the word into a search engine or spelling checker. Or quickly find the word in a dictionary and provide the spelling on the whiteboard. Have the students cross-check their spelling against the spelling you provide. If they spelled the word incorrectly, have them spell the word correctly next to the word that is incorrect.

Provide multiple opportunities to practice this strategy. Reteach it on a regular basis. Every two or three weeks, give a quick ten-minute model and guided practice session on this strategy. You can do it during your dedicated spelling time, but you can also do it as a writing minilesson. Writing instruction time is the perfect time to teach, model, and practice spelling strategies.

Another part of this lesson set can involve teaching students the routine of using flip folders. Instructions for how to construct and use them are in the next chapter. Flip folders help kids store words in the dictionaries in their brains. The folders also teach students a routine they can use during independent writing time: See the word in your mind, write the word, check to see if it looks right, and double-check the spelling by consulting a spelling checker, search engine, teacher, peer, or dictionary.

Finally, consider this: Whereas one child may easily store a word in his or her brain and then "see" it when it comes time to spell it during writing (or a test), another child may not. Even repeated exposures to a word may not be enough to fully encode a word into someone's brain dictionary. If you have students who cannot easily store words in their heads (and later "see" them), encourage them to use strategies that play to their strengths, such as spelling by analogy, thinking about word meaning, and even circling the word and using a spelling source to correct it.

Teaching "Think About Meaning"

Overview

Just as words have sound parts (phonemes) and letter parts (graphemes), they have meaning parts (morphemes). One-syllable words are often morphemes unto themselves. Think about words that rhyme or sound similar, such as *two* and *too*, or *our* and *hour*. Even at a young age, students can be taught to pay attention to the meaning of these words and their appropriate spelling. But the initial teaching must be direct and explicit, and some children will need lots of opportunities to practice.

Think about meaning

In the upper grades, affixes and Greek and Latin roots take center stage. It's at this point that teaching students to pay attention to meaning really pays off. Through the exploration of Greek and Latin roots and root words, children come to understand that word parts contribute to word meanings. By examining the meaning parts of words, children can begin to see how and why they are related, even when at first glance they seem to be unrelated. To see examples of apparently dissimilar words that are actually connected through meaning, such as *asterisk* and *disaster* or *quarter* and *quarantine*, see *Super Spellers*.

Spellings of roots and bases often remain stable across word derivations, even as the sound of the roots and base words change. This is true of words such as *wild* and *wilderness*, *know* and *knowledge*, and *say*, *says*, and *said*. Using meaning to spell an unknown word is a bit like using a chunk or pattern to spell a word you don't (spelling by analogy). A familiarity with affixes and roots can help kids spell words such as *misinformation* and *nondisclosure*. And because encoding (spelling) is the flip side of decoding (reading), all this attention to patterns and words helps students, especially those who struggle, become better readers.

Teaching

As with other spelling strategies, model your thought process as you use this strategy. After you provide modeling, give multiple opportunities to practice it, beginning with guided practice and moving to independent practice. Practice using homophones, such as *their* and *there* or *grown* and *groan*; words that have a similar sound, such as *compliment* and *complement*; and words with multiple meaning parts, such as *uniformity* (*uni* = one, *form* = shape, *ity* = condition of).

Gathering data during writing and spelling will help you decide if students need more practice with the strategy. If they do, provide them with more "think-alouds," as well as guided and independent practice opportunities. Perhaps your class will need a ten-minute model and guided practice session every few weeks.

Here is language for modeling spelling a word by thinking about its meaning:

> **Teacher:** I am going to model how I use the "Think About Meaning" strategy to spell a word that isn't on my spelling list. Let's say I want to spell the word *inescapable* because I am writing, "My situation was inescapable."
>
> The first thing I do is say the word. *"Inescapable."* Saying the word helps me hear its parts. And hearing the parts might enable me to spell a long word I don't know.
>
> Now, I'm going to write the word parts as I think about their meaning. I know the word means something like "you cannot escape." So, I'll start by writing *escape*. I know how to spell that word! And then I'll add the prefix *in*, which means "not or no." Now I have the word *inescape*, which literally means "no escape."
>
> I've never heard anyone say *inescape* and don't think I've ever seen that word written, but I know I've heard and read *inescapable* many times, as in "The prison was inescapable" or "He had reached an inescapable conclusion." So, I'm going to keep going and add the last word part, *able*. In the word it sounds like "uh bull," but I know "uh bull" is really *able*, *a-b-l-e*, which means "condition of." I also know that on most words that end with *e*, I drop the *e* and add the ending. So, I take off the *e*, and add *able* to *inescape* and now I have *inescapable*, which means "a condition of no escape."
>
> Finally, to check and make sure that I have it spelled correctly, I'm going to type the word into a Word document and do a spelling check. Or, I can type it into a search engine or look it up in the dictionary.

Teaching "Use a Mnemonic (Make a Memory Aid)"

Overview

Make a memory aid

I have an especially hard time committing words to my brain dictionary if they originate in a language such as French (*silhouette*) or have strings of consonants and vowels pronounced in an atypical way (*conscientious*). For words I can't see in my mind or break down into common sound-spelling letter patterns, I use a mnemonic.

A mnemonic device is a memory aid. It tricks the mind into remembering and recalling information. The trick can take the form of a clever saying, an acronym, a way of saying a word in a funny way, or a picture or diagram. All of these make something hard to remember easier to remember. At least a few of your spelling lessons should be devoted to teaching students how to generate mnemonics for words that they commonly misspell. If you find that mnemonic devices are helpful to some of your students, keep teaching the strategy.

Instruction begins with teaching students to be metacognitive. They must be aware that some words will be difficult for them to spell. Next, they must identify these difficult words. If you regularly teach students metacognitive reading strategies, such as visualizing or activating prior knowledge, they will be familiar with monitoring their thinking.

Once students know they should be monitoring their frequently misspelled words, and once they have identified words that are difficult for them to spell, teach them how to create a mnemonic. Although you can teach one mnemonic to your entire class, it's better to let students come up with their own way of remembering a word. Individualized mnemonics work best, because what makes sense to one student won't make sense to another. A mnemonic can take any shape or form, as long as its usage results in a correctly spelled word.

One trick is to come up with a phrase that provides a path for spelling a word. Examples of this trick include "Be a *fri*end to the *end*" and "The *principal* is your *pal*." Another trick is to say a word "in a silly way." By silly, I mean to pronounce silent letters, unaccented syllables, and non-English-based words as if they followed typical, common English pronunciations. A third mnemonic is to create mental pictures that remind a speller how to spell a word or word part. The following examples of teacher language give ideas for teaching two of the three tricks just mentioned.

Teaching "Say It a Silly Way"

By now you probably know that teaching a spelling strategy involves modeling your thought processes, giving students multiple opportunities to practice the strategy, and moving from guided practice to independent practice. Here is language for the modeling component of this teaching sequence.

> **Teacher:** When I have a word I consistently misspell, I sometimes "say it in a funny way." This helps me remember how to spell it. For example, I often misspell *environment*. There is a silent letter in the word that throws me off. When I spell the word like it sounds—en-vi-ro-ment—my spelling checker tells me I'm wrong. The correct way to spell the word is en-vi-ron-ment. There is a silent *n* in there! This is because the root word of *environment* is *environ*, which means "surrounding."
>
> To remember how to spell the word with the *n*, I think of my friend Ron, *R-o-n*, who likes to be out in the woods. Whenever I spell *environment*, I think of Ron. This helps me remember to spell the word en-vi-ron-ment. I can even say it in a funny way, "Envi-RON-ment." But I know the real way to pronounce it is "environment."
>
> Here's another example of how I use a mnemonic to spell a word correctly. To spell the word *camouflage* correctly, I pronounce it "cam-oo-flage." This helps me remember there is an *ou*, as in *you*, in it. And I pronounce *flage* like *rage*, because I know how to spell rage, *r-a-g-e*.

Teaching "Make a Picture"

> **Teacher:** To remember how to spell difficult words, I often use a trick called a mnemonic. I already showed you how to say the word in a funny way. Today I am going to model a different spelling trick. I am going to show you how I create a picture. Each part of the picture tells me how to spell part of a word that's difficult to spell.
>
> The word *silhouette* always trips me up. If I spelled it like it sounds, I would spell *s-i-l-l-u-w-e-t*. I definitely know that spelling is wrong. So, I can't use sound to spell this word, and I can't seem to see this word in my head. I need another strategy. I'm going to come up with a picture in my mind. The picture is a boy standing by a house tossing a silver coin and talking to a majorette with brunette hair.
>
> To spell *silhouette* I first think of silver. *S-i-l*. Next, I think of the house. *H-o-u*. Then I think of the majorette with brunette hair. *E-t-t-e*. I put the parts together and get *silhouette*. When I put that word into a search engine, voilà! My spelling is correct.
>
> Here is another example. [Teacher draws a stick figure dancing next to a clock that reads ten o'clock.]
>
> I sometimes forget how to spell *attendance*. If I spell it like it sounds, I write *a-t-e-n-d-e-n-c-e*. I know this is incorrect. So, I draw a picture and remember this phrase: "**At ten**, I can **dance**." When I put *at*, *ten*, and *dance* together, I get *attendance*. When I look up this word in the dictionary, I find I have spelled it correctly!

Teaching "Circle, Come Back, Correct"

Overview

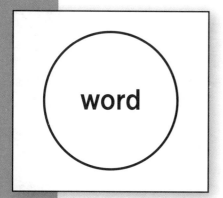

Circle, come back, correct

The "Circle, Come Back, Correct" strategy pulls self-monitoring, correcting misspelled words, and engaging in extended writing into one neat package. When students use the Circle, Come Back, Correct strategy, they demonstrate that they are aware of their spelling mistakes and show they have the ability to purposefully correct a misspelled word. The strategy uses the following sequence:

1. If, while writing, you come to a word you don't know how to spell, spell it as best you can using a spelling strategy that you know.
2. Circle that word.
3. Keep writing.
4. Come back to the circled word at a later time and correct it.

The same sequence holds true when someone thinks a word is spelled correctly but isn't 100 percent sure.

1. If, while writing, you write a word that you think is probably correct (but aren't sure about), circle it.
2. Keep writing.
3. Come back to the circled word and verify that it is correct.

I suggest teaching this strategy in two parts. To do this, you will first need to model writing a short paragraph. Then consider the following two lessons.

Lesson A: Get Close, Circle, Keep Writing

Show your students that when you encounter a word that is difficult to spell, you spell it the best you can. That means you use a strategy such as "Hear and Spell the Sounds" or "Spell by Analogy (Use a Word You Know)" and then circle it. In addition, model how you reread a piece of writing, looking to find other words that might be misspelled. The following bullets give language you can use as you teach this strategy:

- "Writers sometimes don't know how to spell the words they want to write. If you struggle to spell words, don't worry. And don't spend too much time trying to figure out the spelling. Spell the word the best you can and circle it. Then keep writing. At first, it's important to focus more on writing and less on spelling. This is because writers work to write down their thoughts while they are still fresh in their minds."

- "Watch me. I am going to write a short paragraph. [Start to write on a topic of choice.] Now let's say I want to write the word _____ but don't know how to spell it. What can I do? If I want to write a word I don't know how to spell, and if I can't see that word in my head, then I spell it the best I can. I can spell it by hearing and spelling the sounds, spelling it with a pattern I know from another word, or thinking about the meaning of the word. Now I am going to circle this word. [Circle it.] Finally, I keep on writing."

- "When I am finished with my writing, I go back and reread my piece for spelling. I circle any additional words that don't 'look right' to me."

- "Today, when you are writing, use the circle-the-word strategy. If you don't know how to spell a word, spell it the best you can and then circle it. Next, keep on writing."

- "When you are finished writing, go back and reread your piece for spelling. Circle any words that don't 'look right' to you. Circle any words you think might be spelled incorrectly."

Lesson B: Come Back and Correct

After you have taught your students to monitor their spelling and circle words that may not be spelled correctly, teach and let them practice the skill of coming back to circled words and correcting them, or verifying that they are correct. Here are six pieces of language you can use as you guide children to correct or verify their spellings. You will need to directly and explicitly teach students how to do each one.

1. "Cross-check the sounds you hear in the word with the letters and patterns you have written. Stretch your syllables so that you hear all the sounds. Check your word: Are you spelling all of the sounds?"

2. "Cross-check the patterns and syllables you hear in the words with patterns and syllables you know from other words. Can you use a word you already know to get close to the word you don't know?"

3. "Look up the word in a dictionary as best you can or see if the word is on our classroom's list of Writing Words. Ask a friend if the word you have found is in fact the word you are trying to spell."

4. "Type the word into a spelling checker or search engine."

5. "If you can't find the word in the dictionary, or if the spelling checker gives you a word that you know is not the word you want, try spelling your word a different way. Think about your patterns and about spelling by analogy."

6. "If you are still stuck, ask a friend how to spell the word. As a last resort, ask me."

If you teach kindergarten or first grade, having children circle words and then look them up in a dictionary is *not* the best strategy. Simply provide the correct spelling of the word for your students. This can be done with underwriting (see Figure 5.4 in *Super Spellers* for an example of this).

It is appropriate for older students to look up words in a writer's dictionary or the spelling section of a writing journal. A regular dictionary works, too, but if students struggle with this task, scale back and use a writing dictionary or other simplified tool. If a student is working hard to get close to a correct spelling but it is still too far off for the word to be easily found in a writing dictionary or corrected by a spelling checker, then simply provide the correct spelling. I suggest a "not too loose, not too tight" philosophy. You want your students to take responsibility for using strategies and trying to correct their misspellings, but you don't want to frustrate struggling readers by having them plow through a dictionary of words they can't read to find a word they don't know how to spell!

At first, your students may fail to use the "Circle the Word and Correct It" strategy, especially if you have been spelling unknown words for them. But don't lose heart. Keep modeling the strategy, keep your expectations high, and don't give in to automatically spelling words for them when they ask, "How do you spell _____?"

If you have children who regularly spell 99 or 100 percent of their written words correctly, ask them to circle at least two words just to practice the strategy, and challenge them to use more advanced, interesting, and difficult-to-spell words in their writing. Finally, you may have to set a basement or a ceiling on the number of words circled. For the student who misspells many words but never circles any, provide a minimum number of words to aim for, such as, "I expect to see four words circled in every piece of writing." And set a limit for the student who circles ten or fifteen words so they're not focusing exclusively on this strategy. Perhaps you could say, "You are working very hard to practice our strategy. Thank you for your effort. But I want you to practice using only five words. If you circle and correct five words, I know you are really trying."

Teaching students to use spelling strategies gives them power. When students have strategies at their disposal, they have new ways to study their spelling words and then spell them correctly on their weekly spelling tests. More importantly, they have tools for spelling all the words they want to use in writing but aren't sure how to spell. Strategy instruction helps children know that one or more of their spellings might be incorrect, as well as understand they are obligated to fix their errors to the point of total accuracy or confirm that other words are indeed correct.

If students . . .	The teacher can . . .
fail to circle any words in their writing,	say, "I don't see any words circled. What are my expectations for circling words during writing?" say, "I expect you to circle three words in every piece of writing."
don't have misspellings because they are accomplished spellers,	say, "I'd like you to find three simple words that can be replaced with better, more interesting and complex words. Put these three more interesting and complex words into your writing. Circle them. Then look them up and make sure they are spelled correctly."
circle ten, fifteen, or even twenty misspelled words in a piece of writing,	say, "I appreciate that you are taking responsibility for your spelling. I applaud your effort! I want you to concentrate on five important misspelled words. So from now on, circle the five most important words and correct them."

Spelling strategies are the ultimate in teaching students *how* to spell, not *what* to spell. Reflecting on our own writing and spelling can help us understand how important this idea is. When I think about my writing and spelling, I know I don't have strong mental representations for many words. *Rendezvous, ridiculousness, treacherous,* and *rapscallion* are four examples that quickly come to mind. When I take a moment to be metacognitive—to notice my thinking—I notice that as I type those four words, I'm not spelling them effortlessly. Rather, my brain is thinking, *What letters go with the sounds?* and *What spelling pattern should I plug in here?* Also, I am using technology that allows me to "get close and then correct." As I type this paragraph, my Microsoft Word spelling checker is automatically correcting *rendezvous* and *treacherous.* Why? Because I misspelled them! And why did I misspell them? Because they are not yet stored in my mental lexicon. Here's my point: If a fifty-four-year-old author of a spelling book needs strategies to spell, doesn't it make sense that students in elementary school need them as well? The answer to this rhetorical question is yes! So, let's make it our mission to give children what they need: spelling strategies.

CHAPTER 2

Spelling Centers That Support Strategies

Introduction to Spelling Centers

Literacy instruction is most effective when its various "parts" create synergy: Spelling instruction strengthens reading skills, reading instruction supports the development of writing proficiency, writing instruction leads to fluent spelling, and so forth. Synergy occurs between parts, but it also happens within a part (such as spelling). Thus, the upcoming spelling centers support the development of the spelling strategies described in Chapter 1 and the acquisition of spelling features outlined in the lesson sets of Chapters 3 and 4.

Effectively designed spelling centers or workstations provide opportunities for students to use their spelling strategies, make connections to reading and writing, strengthen their orthographic processing systems, and practice their independent work habits. In other words, a well-designed spelling center is a win-win-win-win.

The following spelling centers provide opportunities for children to spell by hearing sounds and assigning letters, by noticing and using patterns, and by seeing the words in their heads. The centers have kinesthetic components, are fun as well as effective, and are mostly low tech. They also come with accountability options, ranging from traditional paper-and-pencil reporting to reporting via electronic tablets and apps such as Seesaw and ClassDojo. Kids being kids, many have a tendency to veer off task. Thus, it's a good idea to have some accountability options at your disposal.

As with all centers, you'll need to explicitly and directly teach your students the purpose, routines, and expectations. I suggest that you then give them guided practice time. If you do this in a whole-group setting, you can monitor the group to make sure everyone is learning the routines correctly. I also suggest that you introduce one center at a time. Introducing centers one at a time, as well as giving students multiple opportunities to practice each one to the point of mastery, helps promote on-task behavior. This behavior is necessary if you are going to effectively teach small groups while the majority of your kids are in centers, spelling or otherwise. And speaking of small groups, varying the content of these spelling centers will allow you to differentiate them to fit the needs of particular groups, meaning multiple groups of students with various achievement levels can use the same center.

How do students work in the centers? It's up to you. Here are some possibilities:

- Students work independently at their desks.
- Students work independently at a word study area.
- Students work with a buddy in either setting.

Additionally, center time can be whole-group time, in which every child picks (or is assigned) a center and uses it for ten to fifteen minutes, or independent work time, done while you are instructing a small group in guided reading, guided writing, or a reading intervention program.

One last note: My philosophy about literacy centers is "Keep it simple 'cause I'm up to my ears in work!" In the classroom, I don't want to deal with complex centers that demand lots of attention. Nor do I want to replace old centers with new ones on a biweekly basis. With this in mind, each spelling center has one basic design, regardless of the grade level it is used in and the content that appears in it. All you need to do is rotate new content into a center at the appropriate times, regularly refresh the supplies of some basic materials (blank and lined paper, colored pencils, word cards, and so on), and collect and briefly scan some of the student work that is generated.

Flip Folder

Easily constructed, and designed for instant error correction, a flip folder gives students in all grades the opportunity to practice the "See the Word in Your Head" strategy.

Materials needed for a flip folder center

- Two manila flip folders (see blackline master in Appendix D)
- Pencils
- Word cards made of card stock with spelling words printed on them. Word cards for this center can be the word-sorting cards presented later in the lesson sets of this book, or you can create your own cards (by hand or digitally) that match the spelling feature of your lesson.
- Blank slips of white paper
- Two laminated direction sheets (see blackline master in Appendix D)

Making Flip Folders

Take a 9-by-11½-inch manila folder and lay it out horizontally so that the "tab" is on the bottom and the top cover of the folder opens upward. Measure down eight inches from the folder's spine and cut off the bottom section of the folder, which includes the tab. You should now have an 8-by-11½-inch folder. Draw a vertical line down the middle of the top cover. Then cut along this line from the bottom to the top. Now you have two flaps, one left and one right. From the blackline master, cut out the directions for the left flap and right flap and glue the directions onto the appropriate flap. If you want the flip folder to last longer, laminate it and then slice open the lamination so you have two working flaps.

Using Flip Folders

First, a student chooses a word card. He says the word, sees it in his mind while reading it, and places the card under the left flap of the flip folder (see Figures 2.1a and 2.1b). Next, the student raises the right flap of the folder, chooses a blank slip of paper from the blank slip pile, puts the slip down on the flip folder's right side, and writes the spelling word (see Figure 2.1c). Finally, the student raises the left flap and compares the spelling word on the word card with the spelling he has just completed (see Figure 2.1d). If the word is spelled correctly, he places a check or

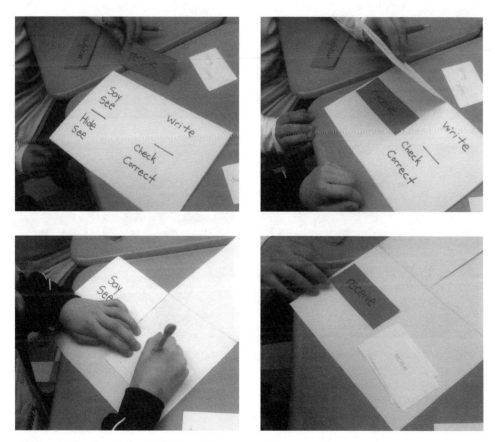

Figures 2.1a (Top Left), 2.1b (Top Right), 2.1c (Bottom Left), 2.1d (Bottom Right)
Flip Folder Photos

a star on it. If the word is spelled incorrectly, the student immediately corrects it. Once the student completes the routine, he repeats it for as many words as he or the teacher desires.

Accountability

- The student clips his spelling slips together, writes his name on the top slip, and puts the stack of word slips into the classroom work basket.

Word Tumble

Manipulating foam blocks is an engaging activity because it is kinesthetic. When the blocks have letters on them, students can spell words, notice patterns, and decide which words are real and which are nonsense (make-believe). (See Figures 2.2a and 2.2b.) The activity also works for onset and rime word chunks (or families).

Figures 2.2a (Top Left), 2.2b (Top Right), 2.2c (Bottom Left), 2.2d (Bottom Right)
Word Tumble Photos

Materials needed for word tumble center

- Blank foam blocks and a black fine-tip marker. Print letters (consonants, digraphs, and vowels), rime patterns (such as *ack, ip, eam*), and even suffixes and prefixes on the foam blocks (see Figure 2.2c and 2.2d). If possible, print consonants and digraphs on blocks of one color (such as blue) and vowels and/or rime patterns on another color (such as red).

- You can also construct card stock or even cardboard blocks from the template in Appendix E. If you go with this method, print the letters and/ or word parts in each square before you assemble and tape or glue each 3-D cube. If possible, print consonants and digraphs using one color (such as blue) and vowels and/or rime patterns using another color (such as red).

- Lined paper and pencil

- Clipboard (if children are on the floor and need a writing surface)

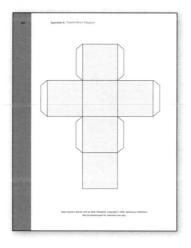

Tumble Block Template

Making Word Tumble

Foam blocks with printed letters and patterns can be purchased from companies that produce educational materials and online, but I prefer to make my own blocks using a blank foam block and a felt-tip marker. This way, I can fine-tune the letters, letter combinations, and patterns I want to present to students. Blank foam blocks can be purchased from Premium Joy, EduPlay, Click N' Play, and other companies.

You decide what spelling blocks to give to your students based on their level of spelling development and the spelling features you have studied in class. Here are some options:

- Individual sounds, letters, and digraphs: *s-p-o-t, l-i-ck, f-l-oa-t, c-ou-ch*

- Mixed letter and pattern level: *f-ind, b-old, b-arn, y-arn, f-l-ing, f-l-y-ing* (or *fl-y-ing*), *c-ove, s-t-ove,* (or *st-ove*)

To limit the number of errors that can occur while spelling and reading words, use previously taught letters and patterns that your students are familiar with but still need to practice.

Using Word Tumble

Depending upon the age and ability of your students, they take turns tumbling three to five blocks. This activity works best if it is done on the floor, not on a desk or table where the blocks can fly off. Students combine the blocks to form as many words as they can. As they form the words, they read them and determine if they're real or nonsense. If the block tossing becomes too vigorous, consider giving the kids a mat with a big circle on it and the expectation that they will toss the blocks inside the ring.

Accountability Options

- Students read the words they make into a recorder.
- Using an electronic tablet, camera, or phone, students take a picture or pictures of the words they form.
- Students record one tumble (toss blocks → form words → read words) with an electronic tablet. Then they post the tumble and the words they made to Seesaw (http://seesaw.me), ClassDojo, or another digital classroom platform.
- After tumbling the blocks, a child picks three words she made, writes them on a piece of paper, and turns in the paper.

Word Hunt and Scavenger Hunt

Students connect spelling to reading by looking for words that use spelling patterns discussed in spelling class. A word hunt is easier to do, but a scavenger hunt works well for older students. Both are engaging ways to review previously studied spelling features. For young students, limit the number of features to look for. Older kids can look for five or six categories of words. Like most activities in school, a word hunt is more fun (and engaging) if it's done with a buddy.

Materials needed for word hunt center

- Previously read text, such as a favorite book
- Sheet of paper, word hunt form, or scavenger hunt form
- Pencil
- Clipboard

 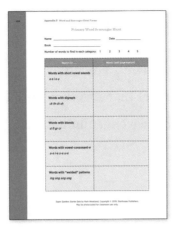 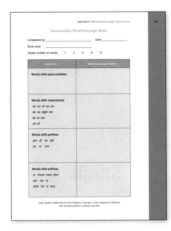

Word- and Scavenger-Hunt Forms

Making Word Hunts or Scavenger Hunts

You don't need much to make this center. First, stock the center with books that your students are familiar with and reflect a wide range of reading levels. You can also encourage your students to bring their favorite book to the word hunt center. Then give them a spelling feature to search for by writing the feature on a blank piece of paper or on the form in Appendix F.

If you want to widen the search and have the kids go on a scavenger hunt for multiple features, use one of the scavenger hunt forms in Appendix F. Highlight the number of words you want in each category. Then highlight the specific spelling features you want them to find. You can also make your own form, crafting it to track exactly what you have taught in spelling. The more expansive you make it, the less often you will have to update it!

Using Word Hunt/Scavenger Hunt

Students search for words that follow the spelling pattern of the week or find patterns from a recent lesson. If students choose to work independently, they can pick any independent reading book. If they choose to work with a buddy, they can each work with a different book or choose multiple copies of the same book (see Figure 2.3). If children work well together, they can also share the same, single book.

Figure 2.3 Students on a word hunt

Accountability Options

- Read the words they find into a recorder.
- Turn in a competed paper that gives book title(s) and a list of words.
- Turn in a word hunt or scavenger hunt form.

Spelling Teacher

Kids love to be the boss (i.e., the teacher), so engage them by putting them in charge. This center lets students practice their strategies and review their spelling words as they spell words on a practice test.

> ### Materials needed for spelling teacher center
>
> - Two clipboards
> - One pencil
> - One red pen
> - Spelling list of eight to sixteen words, appropriate for spelling level of student pairs
> - Two yellow highlighters, two blue highlighters
> - Blank sheets of paper
> - "Teacher" props such as glasses, clip-on tie, and so on (optional)

Making Spelling Test

To start this center and keep it up and running, you only need to gather some basic materials and then keep it stocked with sheets of paper. Even if you have an established center area, clipboards are a good idea because they let kids keep their answers to themselves, as well as scatter throughout the room (if you allow that). The highlighters are for highlighting four words at a time. Having four words fosters turn taking. The red pen is for the test taker to make corrections or for drawing stars. For younger students, the teacher props are optional but fun!

Using Spelling Test

Each student puts his or her word list on a clipboard. Then each child highlights four words on the list with a yellow highlighter. These are the words each child will give (as the teacher) for the spelling test. Next, one child puts the list aside and becomes the student. The other child becomes the teacher.

The teaching child gives his first highlighted word and the student writes down the spelling. You may want to teach the student giving the word to put a check mark next to the highlighted word once he has said it.

When the student has spelled the first word, she puts down the pencil and picks up her pen. Next, the teaching child orally spells the word and the test-taking student either puts a star down or corrects mistakes. It's important that the correction be instant (right after the word is initially spelled). The routine is repeated until the four highlighted words have been given.

Once the teacher has finished dictating four words, he puts down his clipboard and becomes the student. The other child, who is now the teacher, picks up her clipboard and dictates her first highlighted word. The routine is continued. If time allows, the kids can then highlight four more words on their lists and continue switching roles.

Accountability

- Turn in practice tests to the teacher.

Rainbow Words

Writing the spelling features of words in varying colors allows students to easily see the letters associated with sounds, the patterns that exist within words and between words, and the parts of words that contain meaning.

Materials needed for rainbow words center

- Sharp-tipped crayons, markers, or colored pencils
- Blank white paper
- Spelling lists

Making Rainbow Words

You don't need to make much, because the bulk of this center lies in the routine. Simply keep the center stocked with paper and pens, pencils, markers, or crayons. Word lists can come from the child's take-home word list, the lists you might be using from the lesson sets in this book, or a class master list you've curated (see *Super Spellers* or my blog posts on the master spelling list).

Using Rainbow Words

A student writes spelling words from the list in colors, one color for each different spelling feature. You will have to model how to do this and decide the level of spelling development you want your students to work on. Also, you'll need to model exactly the type of word "analysis" you want them to do. Options include the following:

- Writing words at the individual sounds and letters level, as in *s-p-o-t* and *f-l-i-p*. In this instance, students might use one color for the consonants and another color for the vowels (see Figure 2.4a).

- Vowel and consonant digraphs, such as *p-ou-ch*, *ch-ur-ch*, and *b-ar-n-y-ar-d*.

- Writing words on the spoken syllable or pattern level: *barn-yard*, *mi-cro-scope*, *o-ver-ac-tive*. In this example, each syllable would get a different color.

- Writing words on the meaning, root, or root word level: *hunt-ing*, *micro-scope*, *over-active*.

- Words can be written on blank paper in a line, stacked vertically one above the other, or written in the shape of a rainbow. Note that writing words in the shape of the rainbow (as shown in Figure 2.4b) is secondary to the idea of drawing attention to spelling patterns through colors.

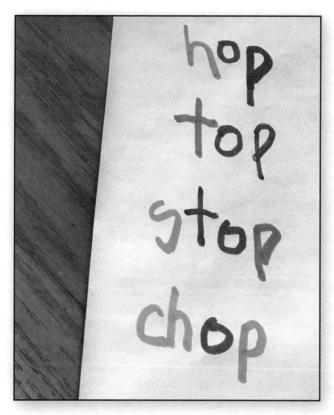

Figure 2.4a Rainbow Words

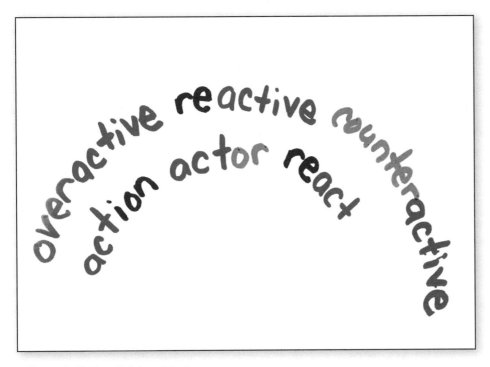

Figure 2.4b More Rainbow Words

Accountability Options

- Write name on paper or template and turn it in.

- Take a picture of the work with an electronic tablet, phone, or camera. If you use ClassDojo or SeeSaw, have the child post their work to their Dojo or SeeSaw account.

Literacy centers or workstations typically help you accomplish a number of important goals. They allow you to differentiate, first by varying a center's content and then by giving you time to meet with differentiated groups for guided reading, guided writing, or an intervention program. They also provide students with multiple opportunities to work on literacy skills, be they spelling, reading, writing, or all three. And centers provide time for students to practice collaboration, as well as to work independently. Both behaviors are critical to a smoothly running classroom.

The best literacy centers (i.e., the most effective ones for both the students and the teacher) allow for student choice (which is motivating and supports success), are based on ongoing routines, are not too difficult for teachers to manage, and support and enrich day-to-day instruction.

The centers in this chapter accomplish all of these goals while hitting all the marks I just listed. Try each one out. Experiment a bit. Observe your students using them. Settle on one or two centers that work especially well for you and your students. And sometime, during the course of a busy day when you happen to glance around the room and see that everything is indeed running smoothly, take a moment to give yourself a pat on the back for a job well done!

CHAPTER 3

Lesson Sets for Teaching Spelling, Grade Band 1–3

Introduction to the Lesson Sets

This book uses the term *lesson sets*. Each set provides you with materials, teaching guidance and language, and a spelling focus for the week or teaching cycle. But because this book is not a spelling program, it does not give fully realized, day-to-day lessons. It will be up to you to introduce the focus as you see fit, choose and possibly adapt the lists, and select which daily activities you will teach.

Every lesson set provided is a model for future lesson sets, ones that you can create using the information and knowledge you gain from this book. Think of this book as a salad buffet. You walk into your kitchen, and voilà, a variety of nutritious salads are laid out in bowls on the countertop. All you need do is decide which salad to choose. But the salad buffet won't last forever. In time you will have to go to your fridge, pull out vegetables, and start making your own. To help you create your own lesson sets, I've provided some tips in a section in Chapter 4 cleverly titled "Creating Your Own Lesson Sets." The section comes at the end of Lesson Set 21.

The same components are found in every lesson set, but again, it will be up to you to decide how you want to introduce the spelling feature, whether you will teach every lesson set component, and how much time you'll give to any particular activity or opportunity for direct and explicit instruction.

Speaking of direct and explicit instruction, I believe this type of teaching is the best starting point (as opposed to beginning with instruction that is based on constructing or discovering meaning). However, what that direct and explicit instruction looks like is mostly up to you. I have given suggestions for teaching language throughout, but the language is not a script, and providing it is not mandated. Finally, even the word lists are guides. Add and subtract words as you see fit. Only you know what works best for your students.

The lesson sets in Chapters 3 and 4 are not based on a specific scope and sequence. Nor are they based on any particular spelling program. They are, however, built on spelling features typically encountered in general grade bands. For example, the first five lessons of Grade Band 1–3 focus on the following: short vowels, consonant digraphs, and long vowels spelled vowel-consonant-*e*. These spelling features are typically taught in first grade. Likewise, the last three lessons of Grade Band 3–5 focus on Greek and Latin roots, spelling features often introduced in fourth and fifth grade.

Why are the lesson sets organized within grade bands and not within a specific grade? Spelling achievement follows a developmental path, not a grade-level path, and students exhibit different levels of spelling mastery within any given grade. Also, different schools group students in different ways. Perhaps you teach a homogenously grouped classroom of twenty fourth-grade students, most of whom are reading roughly two levels behind where they should be. If this is the case, you will want to look in the Grade 1–3 band for appropriate lesson sets. Conversely, maybe you teach high-achieving second graders. These children might be best served by a lesson set in the Grade 3–5 band. For heterogeneously grouped classrooms, I believe it is critical that you identify, through assessments such as spelling and phonics inventories, the achievement level of the majority of your students. You can then differentiate for children above or below this general level.

Regardless of whether students are homogeneously or heterogeneously grouped, there is *always* a continuum of achievement in every classroom. This is why differentiation is necessary. Each lesson set gives ideas for differentiated take-home spelling lists. You can provide further differentiation by offering a variety of spelling activities, writing activities, and spelling centers. Additionally, you can differentiate the content (the words) of centers and activities. This ensures that students at all levels will experience success. Use formative and benchmark data, as well as your teacher sense, to determine which lessons are right for your students.

As you scan through the lessons, remember that this collection of starter sets is just that—a start. It is not a complete program. The goal of this book is to help you come to a specific understanding of how each lesson component works and a general understanding of what types of spelling instruction are best practice. From this point, you can begin to create your own lessons. Ideas and tools for helping you do this are given toward the end of this introduction, at the end of Lesson Set 21 in Chapter 5, and in Appendix I.

Here are descriptions of the components you will find in every lesson set.

Lesson Set Components

Lesson Focus

The lesson focus is the spelling feature(s) you will teach throughout the lesson set. Only two to four features are presented in each lesson. Focusing on this limited number helps students master what you teach, enables you to teach more deeply, and keeps new material at a manageable level for both you and your students.

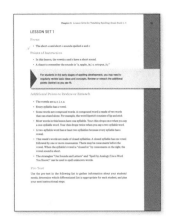

Lesson Set 1

The spelling features presented in the twenty-one lesson sets range from short vowel sounds and vowel teams to consonant-*le* syllables, affixes, and Greek and Latin roots. In many cases, features, such as short vowel patterns, the vowel digraphs *oi* and *ai*, and the prefixes *re*, *de*, and *pre*, are also explained in terms of syllable types, such as closed syllable, vowel-team syllable, and open syllable. For an explanation of the seven syllable types and a deeper conversation about them, see Chapter 5 of *Super Spellers*.

Points of Instruction

Points of instruction explain important aspects of teaching the spelling focus. For example, the focus of Lesson Set 13 is the consonant-*le* spelling. So a point of instruction might sound like this: "The first syllable in most of our *c-le* words has a short-sounding vowel. The short vowel sound is maintained by doubling the consonant. The first syllable ends with a consonant, even though you don't hear it when you say the syllable. If the consonant were not there, the vowel would sound long."

You will notice that many points of instruction contain language on syllable types. If you go to Chapter 5 of *Super Spellers*, you will see a large chunk of text devoted to discussing the syllable types (there are six or seven, depending on how you define them), how they function in spelling and reading, and reasons for teaching them. I suggest teaching both the spelling feature you want to focus on and its corresponding syllable type, with this caveat: Give priority to the spelling pattern. Syllable types can be brought into the instructional mix as additional, secondary ways of understanding spelling patterns. (They also provide additional ways to decode multisyllabic words while reading.) Introduce them cumulatively, not all at once. Finally, if you are unfamiliar with syllable types, then simply leave them out of your instruction until you know more.

How you teach each point of instruction is up to you. I do not offer suggested language here, because I am confident you will find a skillful and effective way to present the main points to your students.

Additional Points to Review or Reteach

Every lesson set offers a list of additional spelling ideas, conventions, and features to review or reteach. The assumption is that you have already covered some or all of these options.

The list changes as the nature of the lesson sets change. In the earlier grade band, options include reteaching vowels or compound words, or reviewing how a closed syllable differs from an open syllable. In the later grade band, options include reviewing the definition of a suffix or prefix and reteaching spelling strategies, such as "Use a Word You Know" and "Circle, Come Back, Correct."

The options are not all-inclusive; you may find that you need to review or reteach something that is not on the list. To decide what you need to teach, gather data at the beginning of the week by giving your students a pre-test and analyzing the errors. Also, take notes on the errors students are making as they read and write. Once you have data on the spelling features students have mastered (or not), adjust your lessons accordingly.

By the way, earlier I mentioned *spelling convention* without defining the term. A spelling convention is whatever is customary or typical. For example, when plurals are formed from words ending in *ch*, *sh*, or *x*, it is conventional to spell the /s/ sound *es*, as in *churches*, *ashes*, and *foxes*. Thus, adding *es* to words ending in *ch*, *sh*, and *x* is a spelling convention. Changing the *y* to an *i* before adding *es*, as in *baby* to *babies*, is also a convention. Conventions are different from spelling features, which we can think of as letters or letter combinations and their associated sounds, syllable types, patterns, suffixes and prefixes, and so on.

Pre-Test and Post-Test Reminders

Toward the beginning of every lesson set is a reminder to give a pre-test, and at the end of every set is a reminder to give a post-test. A pre-test gives you formative information on the features your students have and have not mastered. Based on this information you can determine which differentiated list is appropriate for each student and plan your next instructional steps. A post-test also provides formative information. After giving a post-test, gather information about the spelling features your students have mastered and then plan your next instructional steps. If students did not master the spelling features presented during this instructional cycle, consider reteaching the material in the upcoming cycle.

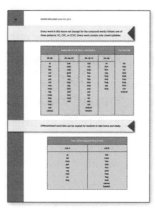

Master Word List

Master Word List

The master word list provides words for your spelling pre-test, your differentiated word lists, your students' take-home lists, your classroom spelling activities, and your end-of-the-week post-test. Feel free to add words that follow the patterns and conventions of each lesson.

As described in *Super Spellers*, a master word list is a list that is narrow and rich. In other words, the words on the master list are based on a limited (narrow) number of spelling features or conventions, but the many words span a continuum of complexity (rich). I suggest teaching two to three features per lesson set for children in the earlier stages of spelling development and three to four features for students in the later stages. This doesn't mean, however, that there are only a few words on a master spelling list. I suggest that each master list consist of at least thirty to forty words and that the words exhibit variety (in their consonant-vowel complexity, number of syllables, types of syllables, and meaning parts) even as they remain rooted in the spelling features you are focusing on.

The words on a master spelling list are to be used for a variety of purposes. Some are used on differentiated spelling lists. Others are used during classroom spelling activities. Still others can be used for the regularly given pre-test or post-test.

A Word About Words

High-frequency words and sight words are typically taught as part of a school's reading, writing, and spelling program. Many teachers and administrators find value in teaching these words and often use a Dolch list as a guide (or as the foundation of their sight-word program). In this book, however, you will *not* find an explicit component in any lesson set that is dedicated to teaching high-frequency words and sight words. There are two reasons for this.

First, the traditional way of teaching these words doesn't play a large part in spelling instruction as I envision it. Reading research shows that the brain's process for reading a word begins with seeing letters, hearing the sounds associated with them, and noticing the similarities and differences between them. The process continues with an unconscious analysis (that includes a statistical "weighting") of word features and their associated pronunciations) and ends with the recognition of the word as a whole (Seidenberg 2016; Ehri and McCormick 2013).

Through this complex process, a word becomes wholly encoded in the brain dictionary, ready for instant recall for spelling. More importantly, a word becomes ready for instant use while reading (by sight, as it were). Because this process is *not* one of strict memorization, in which children repeatedly look at a word in isolation until they remember it, I advocate for high-frequency and sight-word teaching that emphasizes the noticing of patterns. Noticing patterns works best when many words are presented together rather than just one word being presented in isolation.

Second, I assume anyone using this book probably has some type of program available for teaching high-frequency and sight words. Please continue to use whatever method you see fit for teaching your students how to read and write them. If you'd like to know more about my thoughts on the teaching of high-frequency and sight words, please visit my website (www.MarkWeaklandLiteracy.com) and read some of my blog entries on the subject.

Pre-Test List

The purpose of a pre-test is not to give students a test on Monday, have some of them score a 20/20, and then have these advanced spellers take the exact same test again on Friday. Nor is it to give some students the chance to achieve a perfect score on Monday, skip the final test on Friday, and become spelling "tutors" for the remainder of the week. The reasons for giving a spelling pre-test are to determine what your students already know, find out what they don't know, diagnose spelling errors, change your instruction if need be, and differentiate your spelling content for the different levels of achievement you are sure to have in your classroom.

I suggest you give a pre-test on a Monday or at the start of your classroom's teaching cycle. You can give a pre-test of your own design or use the one included in every lesson set. Starting with the established pre-test list might be easiest. Each pre-test list is made up of more and less complex words. Use information generated by your pre-test (and based on your teacher sense) to determine which differentiated word list to give. In time, you'll be able to create your own differentiated word lists for the two or three spelling groups you are running.

Differentiated Word Lists

Two to three lists, ordered from less complex to more complex, are given for each lesson set. Less complex words contain fewer spelling features and/or have fewer letters or syllables than more complex words. I encourage you to eventually create differentiated lists from scratch, or at least modify the provided lists as you see fit. But until you are comfortable doing this, it's fine to give the differentiated word lists as they are.

The word lists are meant to go home with students for study. Based on my experiences, and on talking with other teachers, I would say most parents like the idea of a spelling list coming home. Parents are familiar with the routine of practicing a take-home spelling list, and they feel capable of helping their child study for the test. But satisfying parents is not the reason to give a take-home spelling list. The real reason is to give students one more activity that effectively builds the dictionary in their brain. Spelling lists are a means to an end, with the end being a well-developed lexicon that can be used for fluent reading. Spelling is for reading!

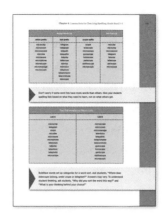

Differentiated Word List

Here's something else to consider: When you give the end-of-the-week spelling test, you can subtract a few words from the take-home list, add a few words, or do both. Students should be prepared to apply strategies to help them spell unstudied words. Remember: Your goal as a teacher is to teach your students how to spell, not simply to give them words to memorize. To build confidence in students, and to give them fair warning, remind them that you are not adding or subtracting words to trick them or make them unsuccessful. Rather, you are changing things to give them the chance to use their strategies. Their goal is to spell unknown words using the sounds and letters, patterns, and meaning parts they already know. My mantra for reinforcing this idea to kids is "If you can spell _____, you can spell _____." So, if *sing* is on their take-home list but on the Friday test I substitute *sting* for *sing*, then I say during the test, "If you can spell *sing*, you can spell *sting*. Spell *sting*."

Finally, I must add that some schools have spelling programs that don't use spelling lists and/or weekly tests. I won't quibble with that type of approach, especially if those schools are producing strong spellers, writers, and readers, but I will say that as I understand it, best practice spelling instruction *includes* a weekly list and a weekly routine of pre-test, study, and post-test (Dunlosky et al. 2013; Allal 1997; Graham 1983).

Look Touch Say

This activity is a nifty way to review letter sounds, syllable types, spelling patterns, word definitions, and much more. Because it constantly cycles back to the basics of what you want to teach, the activity promotes mastery learning. And because it takes only three to four minutes to complete, it makes for a good warm-up before other word-building or word-dictation activities. I've modified and adapted the Look Touch Say routine over the years to make it useful for a variety of teaching situations. Once

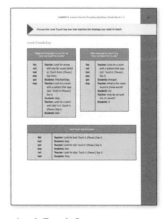

Look Touch Say

you become familiar with it, I think you'll find yourself doing the same.

There are multiple reasons for using this activity. One is to lead kids toward noticing sounds and letters in a word. Another is to have them pay attention to patterns. Still other reasons are teaching them the meaning of words and building their ability to identify words by sight.

Lesson Sets 1–6 and 11–15 include suggestions for Look Touch Say language. Each suggestion spotlights some aspect of spelling instruction: sound-letter association, pattern recognition, learning the meaning of words, words recalled by sight. The suggestions for teaching language are presented in three boxes. The first two contain short routines that you can run on whatever days you choose to do the Look Touch Say process. The third box is an extension, which you can choose to present or not.

Lesson Sets 7–10 and 16–21 do not include suggested language. I believe once you have practiced the language in previous lesson sets, you will be able to easily lead various Look Touch Say routines without having to look at language in this book.

Here are the five ways to think about the Look Touch Say routine:

Type of Routine	Use when you want students to . . .
Word recognition and reading words	practice identifying and reading words.
Hear and spell sounds	practice hearing sounds and noticing how they are represented by individual letters or groups of letters.
See the word in your head	practice seeing the word as a mental construct. They find a word, notice it, close their eyes, see the word in their heads, and then spell it with their eyes closed.
Spell by analogy (use a word you know)	notice patterns within words, remember the patterns, and then use those patterns to spell unknown words (spelling by analogy).
Think about meaning	think about the meaning of words. This language is also used to explore and review vocabulary, which, at the upper grade levels, is intimately entwined with spelling.

Word-Sort Activity

When students sort words, they notice similarities and differences, gain knowledge about how patterns come together to create meaning, and build their mental lexicons (brain dictionaries).

To teach word sorts, start by modeling how the procedure is done. Next, guide the kids as they sort words. Do this as a whole group. Once they learn the sorting routine, as well as the different types of word sorts that can be done, students are ready to work independently or in duos as you monitor their activity and probe their thinking. By *probe* I mean "ask them questions." Their answers will give insight into how they think about word parts, patterns, and meaning. Say, "Tell me why you put those words together." Ask, "Why do you have these words together? How did you decide to create this sort? Could you put this word with that word? Why or why not?"

You'll notice that on each word-sort sheet are two, three, or four words typed in bold. These words are guide words for a closed sort (if you chose to do one). A closed sort is when students are told how to sort the words (as opposed to an open sort that lets students construct meaning and discover relationships for themselves). For

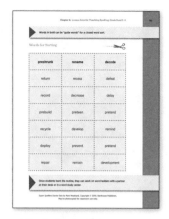

Words for Sorting

example, in Lesson Set 6 the words *pin, pine, tub*, and *tube* are printed in bold. To do a closed sort, tell your students to place those four words in a line across the top of their desks. Then tell them to sort every other word under these four guide words. *Bit* and *rid* would go under *pin, bite* and *shrine* would go under *pine*, and so forth.

Word-sorting activities include closed sorts, open sorts, secret sorts, quick sorts, and sorts using words from multiple lessons. In a closed sort, the teacher names categories for sorting, saying, for example, "Sort your words by the sound patterns *e* as in *Ed* and *o* as in *octopus*" or "Sort your words into two piles, one that contains the suffix *ment* and one that contains the suffix *ness*." A closed sort is directed, and there is little to no debate about where a word belongs.

On the other hand, open sorts are student directed and open to interpretations. Students decide on the categories for sorting, and there can and should be discussion about how and why specific words were grouped together. Your direction for an open sort might sound like this: "Look at your words. Notice how some words relate to one another. Put your words into two, three, or four groups. Make sure you have a reason for grouping words, and be prepared to tell everyone why you put certain words together."

Clopen sort is a term I created because it's fun to say, and, more importantly, it provides a way to think about sorts that are somewhat specific, like a closed sort, but still open to interpretation, like an open sort. For example, the words *pretend, recess, return, decrease, record*, and *defeat* are presented on word cards for word sorting in Lesson Set 16. If I said to my class, "I want you to sort your cards according to spelling patterns you notice," then I am giving them a clopen sort. I didn't give the strict parameters of a closed sort, as in "Sort your cards into three groups by their prefixes." But neither did I give lenient open directions, such as "Sort your cards into groups. Make sure all the cards in each group relate to each other in some way." Here are examples of sorts students might construct based upon the teacher language you use.

I discuss all of these sorts in greater detail in Chapter 6 of *Super Spellers*, where I also define terms such as secret sorts and quick sorts.

Possible Student Sorts					
Closed		**Open**		**Clopen**	
"Sort your cards into three groups by their prefixes."		"Sort your cards into groups. The cards must relate to each other in some way."		"Sort your cards according to spelling patterns you notice."	
defeat decrease	Both have prefix *de.*	return recess defeat record	There are six letters in each word.	defeat decrease	Both have prefix *de*; both have *ea* pattern in second syllable.
return record recess	All have prefix *re.*	pretend	There are seven letters in the word.	return record	Both have prefix *re*; both have *r*-controlled pattern in second syllable.
pretend	Has prefix *pre.*	decrease	There are eight letters in the word.	recess pretend	Both have short-*e* pattern in second syllable.

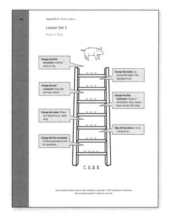

Word Ladders

Word Ladders

Word ladders involve morphing one word into another. Sometimes the word is changed one letter at a time. At other times, digraphs are subtracted or added, vowel teams are swapped in and out, and meaning-making parts are deleted or inserted. A change in one word creates a new word, and each new word is a rung on the ladder. Starting with the word at the bottom of the ladder, it may take a speller five, six, or more words to reach the target word at the top.

At their most basic level, word ladders help children notice sounds, especially inner vowels. Here is a long word ladder that helps spellers notice vowels (notice how each new word changes one spelling feature of the previous word): *cat, cut, cup, pup, pep, pen, pan, pin, pit, pot, hot, hog.* This shorter word ladder also focuses on vowels: *chick, chip, chap, chop, cheap, cheep.*

At a more advanced level, word ladders help children understand meaning. For example, a word ladder clue might say, "Add one letter to *retest* to make a word that means a test taken before a final test." The answer is *pretest.* Here's another word ladder clue that prompts children to think about meaning: "Take the Latin root off *eject.* Add a new Latin root to make a word that means 'to violently break and explode like a volcano.'" The new word? *Erupt.*

As with every activity you teach, present a word ladder to the whole class, model how it is done, and then guide students as they complete a new one. Once students understand the process of doing word ladders, they can do them on their own. And once you get the hang of word ladder construction, you can create your own. They don't need to be fancy and they don't have to have a clever beginning and ending. Another option is to challenge your students to make their own word ladders. Nothing tickles students more than when you present something they created to the entire class.

Word Dictation

Word dictation gives students opportunities to listen, apply strategies, analyze mistakes, and think over the sounds, patterns, and meanings of words. Dictation is most often done with the whole group, but you can also use it as a warm-up in a guided reading or intervention group. The tools for writing words can range from low- to high-tech. Have students write words with paper and pencil, with individual whiteboards and markers, or on digital tablets. Words can also be constructed with letter- and word-family tiles. When it comes to letter and "word chunk" tiles, my favorite product continues to be Wilson Language's Magnetic Journal. However, I've used many other types of tiles over the years and even made my own.

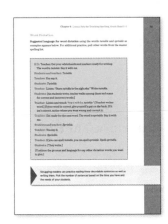

Word Dictation

You will find all the dictation words you need on the master spelling list. Base the words you choose on the needs of your students. Different groups of students can get different words.

Like Look Touch Say, word dictation takes only three to four minutes to complete. Thus, it makes a good warm-up at the beginning of a lesson. It also can be an ending activity. Once students are comfortable with the routine, you can provide pairs of students with a short list of words to dictate to each other during independent work time. And once you learn the routine and the language, you will no longer need to read the activity out of this book. This is why you will find dictation language only in Lesson Sets 1–6 and 11–15.

Sentence Dictation

In sentence dictation, students listen to and then write a sentence that is completely encodable. In other words, every word in the sentence is based on what students are currently learning or have previously learned. Sentence dictation gives children the opportunity to apply spelling strategies across a string of words and asks them to listen closely to an entire sentence, remembering what was said.

Sentence Dictation

The sentence dictation script is based on "I say, we say, you say, you write." This means the teacher says the sentence, the students say the sentence with the teacher, and then the students say the sentence on their own. Only then do they write the sentence. For a sentence to be correct, it must contain both correct spelling and correct mechanics (capitalization and punctuation).

During my spelling presentations, teachers often ask me, "Can I repeat the sentence one more time?" or "Can I go back through the sentence word by word?" The short answer is "Yes, of course." The longer answer is this: The goal of this activity is not to test memory but to have children hear sounds in words across a sentence and then encode those words by writing them. However, there is definitely an element of remembering to this activity, and students are tasked with paying attention. You know your students best. If they need to hear the sentence one or two more times, then repeat it. But if you think they will benefit from the challenge of the unmodified I Say, We Say, You Say, You Write format, then encourage them to pay attention and use the routine as is.

Like word dictation, sentence dictation can take many forms. Students can write with paper and pencil or with a whiteboard and marker. They can also write on a computer tablet using any number of writing apps, but make sure the spelling-check function is deactivated! You can incorporate the activity into your weekly spelling test if you wish. Once you realize how sentence dictation works, make up your own sentences. The trick is to come up with sentences created from spelling patterns that students have either learned to the point of mastery or are practicing in their current spelling lesson. For more on this activity, see Chapter 6 of *Super Spellers*.

A Few Words on Assessing Spelling

My personal belief is that school systems spend way too much time assessing children in ways that fail to inform instruction and lead only to less-than-meaningful grades on a report card, school rankings in the newspaper, and a loss of valuable instructional time. But this doesn't mean assessment isn't necessary. In fact, assessment is an essential part of teaching. How else do you know if your instruction is working?

This book includes assessment tools. There are two strategy survey sheets in Appendix C. And words for a suggested pre-test are given in each lesson set, as are differentiated take-home lists that can be used for post-tests. However, these surveys and lists are recommended, not compulsory. There aren't any direct commands for how you should assess spelling in this book. My assumption is that you teach in a school that has guidelines, parameters, and nonnegotiables regarding assessment. I also assume that you are adept at figuring out how to meet those considerations and directives. Therefore, I believe that you either already know or will soon figure

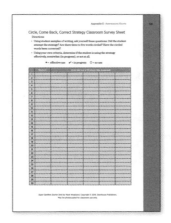

Assessment Sheets

out how to gather spelling data that informs your instruction, gives you information on the growth of each student's spelling ability, and provides scores that can be translated into a spelling grade if your district report card demands it.

I would be remiss, however, if I didn't provide you with some additional support in assessment. Thus, I offer the following thoughts.

Writing Samples

Writing samples provide a wealth of spelling information. When viewed through the lens of assessment, uncorrected student writing samples give information about how students hear and spell the sounds of the English language, use the rules of our grammar system, and apply meaning as they write words and craft sentences.

Options on how to gather and "score" this information are many: You can calculate a percentage (number of misspelled words out of every 100 words); create and label general categories of spelling proficiency (such as zero or one spelling error in a writing sample equals advanced, two spelling errors equals proficient, and three or more errors mean the student needs improvement); calculate the number of spelling errors that children self-identified in their writing and then corrected; assess whether students are using spelling strategies as they write; and so forth.

Regarding the last two, Appendix C gives you assessment sheets for gathering formative information on whether your students are (1) using spelling strategies while writing and (2) finding their spelling errors in their writing and then attempting to correct those misspelled words.

Spelling Activities

Spelling activities generate assessment information. This is especially true of the word- and sentence-dictation activities. You can gather this information and use it to inform instruction, or not. If you do want to gather and use it, collect student word and sentence samples and then analyze them to assess whether your students are mastering sound-letter spelling, pattern spelling, and the use of meaning parts. Samples can take the form of words and sentences written on paper, on a digital platform such as a tablet-based writing program, or through an app such as SeeSaw.

Spelling Lists and Tests

In *Super Spellers*, I say that a traditional summative testing cycle (aka "memorize the list and then move on to a new list") tells children *what* to spell but doesn't do much to teach them *how* to spell. On the other hand, a carefully constructed word list combined with effective spelling instruction, activities, and a test-study-test cycle (which includes a pre-test at the beginning of the cycle and a post-test at the end) does effectively teach children how to spell, and it helps them become better readers and writers. So, go ahead and give that end-of-cycle or end-of-week spelling test. But consider it formative in nature, and remember that rather than being the sole reason for your spelling instruction, a post-test is only one component in an ongoing cycle of spelling instruction.

Data generated from any or all of these three sources—writing samples, classroom activities, and end-of-cycle or end-of-week spelling tests—can be used to produce a spelling grade for a report card. But report card grades demand standardization across classrooms and grade levels. This means you will need to discuss with your fellow teachers and administrators the elements of spelling instruction you will use to generate a grade and how you will calculate various scores.

Making Lesson Sets of Your Own

Scope and Sequence

If you find the spelling instruction presented in this book effective, you'll want to continue with it. To do that, you'll need to make your own lesson sets, each with a spelling focus, a master list, differentiated take-home lists, dictation activities, and so on. To help you do that, consider getting a copy of *Super Spellers: Seven Steps to Transforming Your Spelling Instruction*. *Super Spellers* offers support in developing a spelling scope and sequence, discusses how to choose words for use in a word list, gives additional ideas on word sorts, lists resources for finding words, provides information on the various syllable types, and much more. Additionally, Appendix H of this Starter Set book contains three scopes and sequences of varying complexity. They may be of use as you consider constructing your own lesson sets. Finally, there is a Lesson Planning Template in Appendix I. On the template are all the components of a Super Spellers Lesson Set, including places to create a master list, a pre-test list, sentences for dictation, the important points you want to teach and remember, the words you want to have your students sort, and so forth.

Armed with a strong idea of what you want to teach, a deep and rich pool of words that exhibits specific spelling features, a list of specific teaching strategies, a menu of activities that provide students with spelling practice, and a few basic materials, you will be ready to create your own lessons for any spelling feature or convention you want to teach.

Now, on to the lesson sets!

LESSON SET 1

Focus

- The short-*a* and short-*o* sounds spelled *a* and *o*

Points of Instruction

- In this lesson, the vowels *a* and *o* have a short sound.
- A chant to remember the sounds is "*a,* apple, /a/; *o,* octopus, /o/."

> For students in the early stages of spelling development, you may need to regularly review basic ideas and concepts. Review or reteach the additional points (below) as you see fit.

Additional Points to Review or Reteach

- The vowels are *a, e, i, o, u.*
- Every syllable has a vowel.
- Some words are compound words. A compound word is made of two words that can stand alone. For example, the word *lipstick* consists of *lip* and *stick.*
- Most words in this lesson have one syllable. Your chin drops once when you say a one-syllable word. Your chin drops twice when you say a two-syllable word.
- A two-syllable word has at least two syllables because every syllable has a vowel.
- This week's words are made of closed syllables. A closed syllable has one vowel followed by one or more consonants. There may be consonants before the vowel. When the syllable's vowel is "closed in" by consonants on the right, the vowel sound is short.
- The strategies "Use Sounds and Letters" and "Spell by Analogy (Use a Word You Know)" can be used to spell unknown words.

Pre-Test

Use the pre-test in the following list to gather information about your students' needs, determine which differentiated list is appropriate for each student, and plan your next instructional steps.

Every word in this lesson set (except for the compound words) follows one of three patterns: VC, CVC, or CCVC. Every word contains only closed syllables.

Master Word List: short-*a* and short-*o*				Pre-Test List
at, ap	**ab, ag, ad**	**ob, op, ot**	**on, og**	
at	cab	cob	on	fat
fat	stab	rob	Don	nap
flat	slab	mop	Ron	lot
cat	grab	hop	log	slop
hat	flag	top	hog	stab
pat	rag	flop	dog	trap
sat	bag	slop	frog	frog
nap	tag	stop	jog	Ron
map	bad	pop	slog	not
tap	dad	got		bobcat
snap	had	hot		
flap	mad	lot		
slap	sad	slot		
trap		not		
zap		bobcat		
catnap		hotshot		

Differentiated word lists can be copied for students to take home and study.

Two Differentiated Word Lists	
List A	List B
at	flat
sat	snap
mop	trap
got	slop
nap	Ron
rag	grab
had	frog
on	flag
dog	stab
	catnap
	hotshot

> Choose the Look Touch Say box that matches the strategy you want to teach.

Look Touch Say

Suggested language for practicing "Hear and Spell the Sounds"	
flat not had slap got slop	**Teacher:** Look for words with the /a/ sound (short *a*). Touch them. [Pause.] Say them. **Students:** *Flat/had/slap.* **Teacher:** Look for a word with a pattern that says /ap/. Touch it. [Pause.] Say it. **Students:** *Slap.* **Teacher:** Look for a word with /ad/ in it. Touch it. [Pause.] Say it. **Students:** *Had.*

More language for practicing "Hear and Spell the Sounds"	
flat not had slap got slop	**Teacher:** Look for a word with a pattern that says /ot/. Touch it. [Pause.] Say it. **Students:** *Not/got.* **Teacher:** What is the vowel sound in these words? **Students:** /o/. **Teacher:** How do we spell the /o/ sound? **Students:** *O*

Look Touch Say Extension	
flat bad got slop not had	**Teacher:** Look for *bad*. Touch it. [Pause.] Say it. **Students:** *Bad.* **Teacher:** Look for *not*. Touch it. [Pause.] Say it. **Students:** *Not.* **Teacher:** Look for *slop*. Touch it. [Pause.] Say it. **Students:** *Slop.*

Cut out the words and decide what type of sort the children will do. Will it be open or closed?

Words in bold can be used as sorting guide words or headings. If students use them, they will sort all the words under either *sat* or *hop*.

Words for Sorting

sat	hop
stop	slap
map	snap
dot	crop
hot	frog
cap	flag

Do word ladder activities as a whole group until students learn the routine.
Words are written from bottom to top.

Word Ladder: Turn a Cat into a Dog

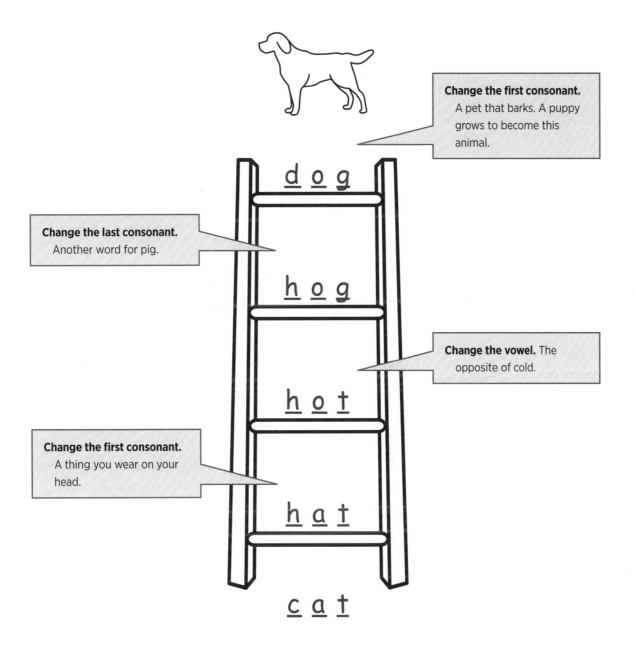

Change the first consonant. A pet that barks. A puppy grows to become this animal.

d o g

Change the last consonant. Another word for pig.

h o g

Change the vowel. The opposite of cold.

h o t

Change the first consonant. A thing you wear on your head.

h a t

c a t

Word Ladder: Turn Dad into a Frog

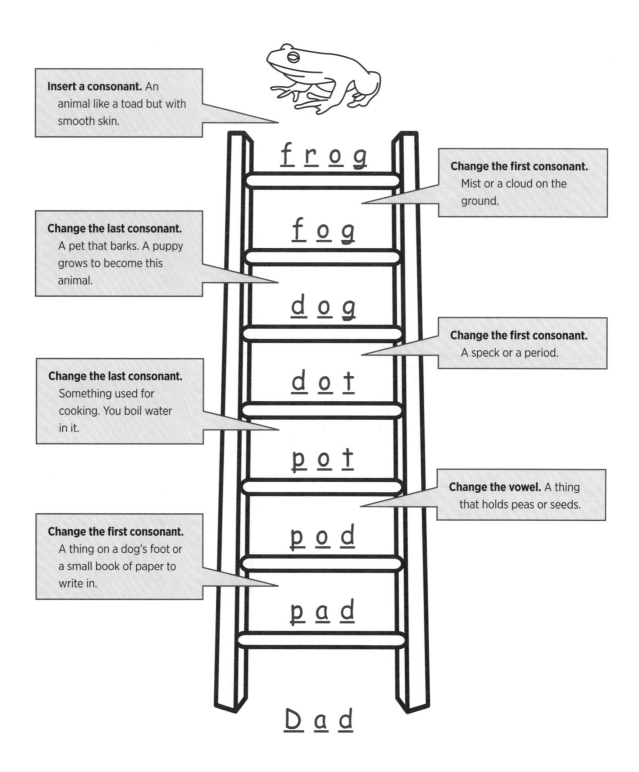

Insert a consonant. An animal like a toad but with smooth skin.

f r o g

Change the first consonant. Mist or a cloud on the ground.

f o g

Change the last consonant. A pet that barks. A puppy grows to become this animal.

d o g

Change the first consonant. A speck or a period.

d o t

Change the last consonant. Something used for cooking. You boil water in it.

p o t

Change the vowel. A thing that holds peas or seeds.

p o d

Change the first consonant. A thing on a dog's foot or a small book of paper to write in.

p a d

D a d

It's a good idea to vary the ways in which students write their words. Have them use whiteboards one week, paper and pencils the next. Encourage spellers to use strategies such as stretching words and zapping sounds.

Word Dictation

Suggested language for word dictation using the words *flat* and *brat* as examples is shown below. For additional practice, pull other words from the master spelling list.

Teacher: Get your whiteboards and markers ready for writing, everyone. The word is *flat*. Say it with me.

Students and teacher: *Flat.*

Teacher: You say it.

Students: *Flat.*

Teacher: Listen: "The tabletop is *flat*." Write *flat*.

Students: [As students write, teacher walks among them and scans for correct and incorrect words.]

Teacher: Listen and watch: "f-l-a-t, *flat*." [Teacher writes word.] If your word is correct, give yourself a pat on the back. If it isn't correct, fix it.

Teacher: Get ready for the next word. The word is *brat*. Say it with me.

Students and teacher: *Brat.*

Teacher: You say it.

Students: *Brat.*

Teacher: If you can spell *flat*, you can spell *brat*. Spell *brat*.

Students: [As students write, teacher walks among them and scans for correct and incorrect words.]

Teacher: Listen and watch: "b-r-a-t, *brat*." [Teacher writes word.] If your word is correct, give yourself a pat on the back. If it isn't correct, fix it.

(Continue the process and language for any other dictation words you want to give.)

Practice spelling one, two, or three sentences. Practice reading four or five. Choose the number of sentences for dictation and reading based on the time you have and the needs of your students.

Sentence Dictation

Sentences for dictation and reading

The fat cat was mad.

That cat is bad.

Matt sat on the log.

The fat hog got mad.

I had a hot dog and pop.

Do not grab a fat hog.

Pop had to hop on the log.

Dad had a mop and a rag.

A dog and a frog sat on a log.

I can snap and tap my fingers.

A frog can hop, and a dog can nap.

Suggested language for sentence dictation using *The fat hog got mad* appears below.

Teacher: Get your whiteboards and markers ready for writing, everyone. The sentence is *The fat hog got mad.* Say it with me.

Students and teacher: *The fat hog got mad.*

Teacher: You say it.

Students: *The fat hog got mad.*

Teacher: Write it.

Students: [As students write, teacher walks among them and scans for correct and incorrect words.]

Teacher: Listen and watch: "The fat hog got mad." [Teacher writes sentence.] If your words are spelled correctly, you started with a capital letter, and you have a correct ending mark, give yourself a pat on the back. If your sentence isn't correct, notice where you went wrong and fix it.

Post-Test

- At the end of your cycle of instruction, test your students by using the appropriate differentiated word list.

- Once you've effectively taught your students how to spell, not what to spell, you have the opportunity to add or substitute a word that isn't on the take-home list. For example, if *slop* was on the list, a student should also be able to spell *crop* or *stop*.

- A post-test provides formative information. After giving the post-test, gather information about your students' needs and plan your next instructional steps. If students did not master the spelling features presented during this instructional cycle, consider reteaching the material in the upcoming cycle.

LESSON SET 2

Focus

- The short-*i* and short-*u* sounds spelled *i* and *u*; the ending /k/ sound spelled *ck*

Points of Instruction

- The vowels *i* and *u* have a short sound when they are followed by a consonant.
- At the end of a one-syllable word with a short vowel sound, the /k/ sound is usually spelled *ck*.
- The letters *ck* make one sound.
- The /k/ sound spelled *ck* never occurs at the beginning of a word.

> For students in the early stages of spelling development, you may need to review basic ideas and concepts. Review or reteach the additional points below as you see fit.

Additional Points to Review or Reteach

- Vowels are the letters *a, e, i, o, u*.
- A chant for short vowel sounds is "*a*, apple, /a/; *e*, Ed, /e/; *i*, itch, /i/; *o*, octopus, /o/; *u*, umbrella, /u/."
- A digraph consists of two letters that make one sound. The letters *ck* are a digraph.
- Every word in this lesson set contains closed syllables. A closed syllable has one vowel followed by one or more consonants. There may be consonants before the vowel. When the syllable's vowel is "closed in" by consonants on the right, the vowel sound is short (with a few exceptions).
- Some words on the list are compound words. A compound word is made up of two words that can stand alone. For example, *bathtub* consists of *bath* and *tub*.
- The strategies "Hear and Spell the Sounds" and "See the Word in Your Head" can be used to spell these words.

Pre-Test

Use the pre-test in the following list to gather information about your students' needs, determine which differentiated list is appropriate for each student, and plan your next instructional steps.

The word *chopsticks* is plural. Consider adding an *s* to other words and teaching the concept of plurals.

The phonograms with asterisks are from the list of thirty-seven high-frequency phonograms.

Master Word List: short-*i*, short-*u*, *ck*				Pre-Test List
in*, ick*, it*	**ip*, id, ig, imp, ist**	**uck*, ug*, ump*, ub**	**up, ust, un**	
it	grip	bug	up	sit
sit	slip	hug	cup	spin
hit	flip	rug	pup	chug
slit	ship	slug	dust	stuck
in	lid	chug	gust	just
pin	did	duck	just	slick
win	limp	muck	must	blimp
shin	blimp	luck	rust	pup
chin	fist	stuck	fun	mist
spin	list	bump	run	twig
sick	mist	jump	sun	duck
tick	big	lump		bathtub
click	pig	cub		lipstick
slick	twig	rub		
stick		bathtub		
lipstick				
chopsticks				

Two Differentiated Word Lists	
List A	**List B**
big	shin
win	slick
chin	blimp
run	stuck
bug	chug
rug	click
duck	must
big	muck
sick	click
click	twig
	chopsticks
	bathtub

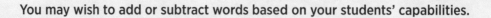

You may wish to add or subtract words based on your students' capabilities.

See Chapter 2 to review the strategies "Hear and Spell the Sounds," "See the Word in Your Head," and others.

Suggested language for practicing word recognition and reading	
win chin run bug rug sick click must	**Teacher:** Look for *win*. Touch it. [Pause.] Say it. **Students:** *Win.* **Teacher:** Look for *bug*. Touch it. [Pause.] Say it. **Students:** *Bug.* **Teacher:** Look for *click*. Touch it. [Pause.] Say it. **Students:** *Click.*

Suggested language for practicing "Hear and Spell the Sounds"	
win chin run bug rug sick click must	**Teacher:** Look for a word with a pattern that says /un/. Touch it. [Pause.] Say it. **Students:** *Run.* **Teacher:** How do we spell the /u/ sound? **Students:** *U.* **Teacher:** Look for words with a pattern that says /in/. Touch them. [Pause.] Say them. **Students:** *Win, chin.* **Teacher:** How do we spell the /i/ sound? **Students:** *I.*

Look Touch Say Extension	
You can include word meaning in your Look Touch Say routine. Here is some suggested language.	
chin run bug rug sick click must	**Teacher:** Look for another word for insect. Touch it. [Pause.] Say it. **Students:** *Bug.* **Teacher:** Look for a word that is a part of your body. Touch it. [Pause.] Say it. **Students:** *Chin.* **Teacher:** Look for a word that means "to pester someone or irritate someone." Touch it. [Pause.] Say it. **Students:** *Bug.*

Words in bold are guide words for a closed sort.

Words for Sorting

sit	**rug**
spin	stuck
must	slick
blimp	pup
lipstick	twig
duck	bathtub

Do word ladder activities as a whole group until students learn the routine.

Word Ladder: Turn a Pig into a Duck

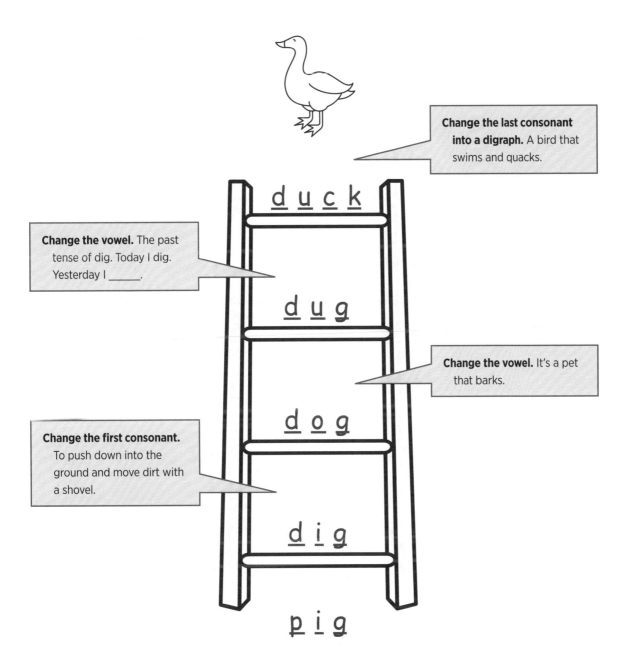

Change the last consonant into a digraph. A bird that swims and quacks.

d u c k

Change the vowel. The past tense of dig. Today I dig. Yesterday I _____.

d u g

Change the vowel. It's a pet that barks.

d o g

Change the first consonant. To push down into the ground and move dirt with a shovel.

d i g

p i g

Word Ladder: Bug on a Twig

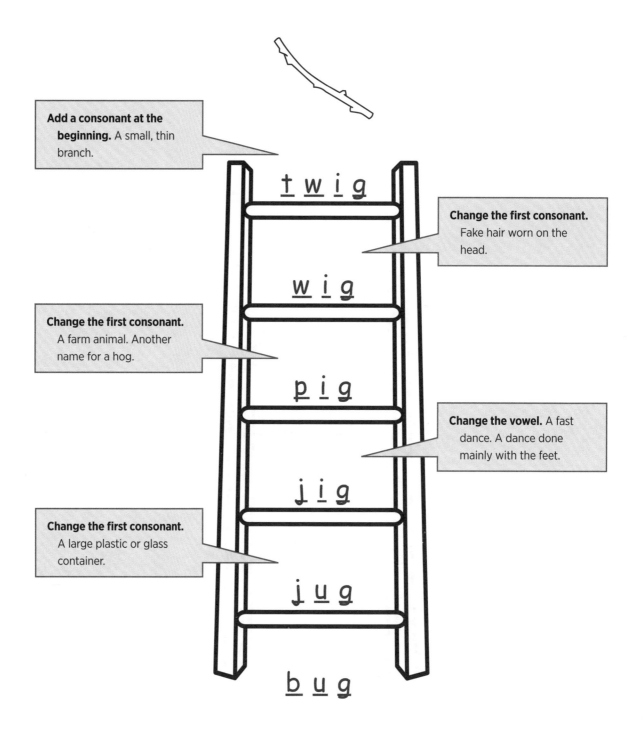

Add a consonant at the beginning. A small, thin branch.

t w i g

Change the first consonant. Fake hair worn on the head.

w i g

Change the first consonant. A farm animal. Another name for a hog.

p i g

Change the vowel. A fast dance. A dance done mainly with the feet.

j i g

Change the first consonant. A large plastic or glass container.

j u g

b u g

More words for this activity can be found in this lesson set's master list. Have students practice whatever words you think are appropriate.

Word Dictation

Suggested language for word dictation using the words *grip* and *slip* as examples appears below. For additional practice, pull other words from the master spelling list.

> Teacher: Get your electronic tablets ready, everyone. The word is *grip*. Say it with me.
>
> Students and teacher: *Grip*.
>
> Teacher: You say it.
>
> Students: *Grip*.
>
> Teacher: Listen: "I have a *grip* on the dog leash." *Grip*. Write it.
>
> Students: [As students write, teacher walks among them and scans for correct and incorrect words.]
>
> Teacher: Listen and watch: "g-r-i-p, *grip*." [Teacher writes word.] If your word is correct, give yourself a pat on the back. If it isn't correct, notice where you went wrong and correct it.
>
> Teacher: Get ready for the next word. The word is *slip*. Say it with me.
>
> Students and teacher: *Slip*.
>
> Teacher: You say it.
>
> Students: *Slip*.
>
> Teacher: If you can spell *grip*, you can spell *slip*. Spell *slip*.
>
> Students: [They write.]
>
> (Continue the process and language for any other dictation words you want to give.)

If you do not teach syllable types (such as closed, open, *r*-controlled), omit the term *closed syllable* from the suggested language.

Sentence Dictation

Sentences for dictation and reading

Did the lid fit?

Tab had a sip.

Matt had a rash.

Hand Mom the cups.

Bob and Sid sat in the sun.

Get a grip on the rug or you will slip.

Sid sat in a big bathtub.

The bug sat on a stick in the pit.

A frog can jump and swim.

Rick and Kim got a bag of chips.

Did you see the dog jump off the blimp?

I lick and smack my thick lips.

Suggested language for sentence dictation using *I smack my thin lips* appears below.

Teacher: Get your whiteboards and markers ready for writing, everyone. The sentence is *I smack my thin lips*. Say it with me.

Students and teacher: *I smack my thin lips.*

Teacher: You say it.

Students: *I smack my thin lips.*

Teacher: Write it.

Students: [As students write, teacher walks among them and scans for correct and incorrect words.]

Teacher: Listen and watch: "I smack my thin lips." [Teacher writes sentence.] *Smack* ends with the /k/ sound. In one-syllable closed-syllable words (with a short vowel sound), the /k/ is almost always spelled *ck*.

Post-Test

- At the end of your cycle of instruction, test your students by using the appropriate differentiated word list.

- Once you've effectively taught your students how to spell, not what to spell, you have the opportunity to add or substitute a word that isn't on the take-home list. For example, if *dig* was on the list, a student should also be able to spell *wig* or *twig*.

- A post-test provides formative information. After giving the post-test, gather information about your students' needs and plan your next instructional steps. If students did not master the spelling features presented during this instructional cycle, consider reteaching the material in the upcoming cycle.

LESSON SET 3

Focus

- Double *s*, *f*, and *l* at the end of one-syllable words

Points of Instruction

- The spellings for the sounds /f/, /l/, and /s/ at the end of one-syllable words are *ff*, *ll*, and *ss*.
- Double letters or "bonus" letters occur at the end of one-syllable words that end in *f*, *s*, and *l*.
- When *a* appears with *ll*, the sound of the *a* changes, from /a/ as in *apple* to /aw/ as in *all*.

> The points below give ideas for reviewing or reteaching spelling concepts that have not yet been mastered.

Additional Points to Review or Reteach

- Most words in this lesson have one syllable. Your chin drops once when you speak a one-syllable word. For a two-syllable word, your chin drops twice.
- One-syllable words ending in double *ff*, *ll*, and *ss* are also closed-syllable words. A closed-syllable word has one vowel followed by one or more consonants. When the syllable's vowel is closed in by consonants, the vowel sound is short.
- Two letters that make one sound (such as *ck*, *sh*, *ll*, and *ff*) are called digraphs.
- The strategies "Hear and Spell the Sounds," "See the Word in Your Head," and "Spell by Analogy (Use a Word You Know)" can be used to spell words in this lesson set.

Pre-Test

Use the pre-test in the following list to gather information about your students' needs, determine which differentiated list is appropriate for each student, and plan your next instructional steps.

Double letters or "bonus" letters occur at the end of one-syllable words that end in *f*, *s*, and *l*. *Ell* and *ill* are from the list of thirty-seven high-frequency phonograms.

Master Word List: double *s*, *f*, *l*			Pre-Test List
pass	Jeff	bell	grass
grass	stiff	fell	mess
less	off	sell	stiff
mess	buff	well	floss
dress	cuff	bill	Jeff
kiss	puff	dill	gruff
hiss	fluff	fill	dill
miss	gruff	gill	swell
boss	huff	pill	spill
loss	stuff	hill	gumball
floss		grill	crabgrass
moss		still	
toss		spill	
fuss		all	
crabgrass		ball	
		gumball	
		softball	

You may wish to add or subtract words based on your students' capabilities.

Two Differentiated Word Lists	
List A	**List B**
pass	dress
less	floss
kiss	stuff
fill	spilling
off	swelling
stuff	grass
hill	tallest
fell	stall
spill	puffball
fall	softball
	address

> Choose the Look Touch Say routine that matches what you want to teach.

Look Touch Say

Suggested language for practicing "Hear and Spell the Sounds"	
all stall dress grass kiss pass stuff off stiff	**Teacher:** Look for words with a pattern that says /all/. Touch them. [Pause.] Say them. **Students:** *All/stall.* **Teacher:** Look for a word with a pattern that says the /iff/ sound. Touch it. [Pause.] Say it. **Students:** *Stiff.* **Teacher:** How do we spell the /f/ sound at the end of a one-syllable word? **Students:** *F-f.*

More language for practicing "Hear and Spell the Sounds"	
ball dress tall grass kiss fluff off	**Teacher:** Look for a word with the /all/ sound. Touch it. [Pause.] Say it. **Students:** *Ball/tall.* **Teacher:** Look for a word with the /s/ sound. Touch it. [Pause.] Say it. **Students:** *Dress/grass/kiss.* **Teacher:** How do we spell the /s/ sound at the end of a one-syllable word? **Students:** *S-s.* **Teacher:** Look for a word with the /f/ sound. Touch it. [Pause.] Say it. **Students:** *Fluff/off.* **Teacher:** What do the words *fluff, grass,* and *ball* have in common? **Students:** They all have double consonants at the end. They all have bonus letters at the end.

Look Touch Say Extension	
Spelling by analogy is a powerful way to spell. Here is suggested language for practicing the analogy strategy using words from this lesson set.	
ball hall mess grass kiss pass fluff off stiff	**Teacher:** Look for a word with the *s-s* pattern. Touch it. [Pause.] Say it. **Students:** *Mess/grass/kiss/pass.* **Teacher:** If you said *mess, grass, kiss,* or *pass,* you are correct. What pattern is shared with these four words? **Students:** *S-s.* **Teacher:** If you can spell *kiss,* you can spell *miss.* Tell your elbow buddy how to spell *miss.* [Children turn and spell.] **Teacher:** Look for a word with the *f-f* pattern. Touch it. [Pause.] Say it. **Students:** *Fluff/off/stiff.* **Teacher:** If you can spell *fluff,* you can spell *gruff.* Tell your elbow buddy how to spell *gruff.* [Children turn and spell.] **Teacher:** Why do *stiff, fluff, mess,* and *hall* have double letters or bonus letters at the end?

Words in bold are guide words for a closed sort. Prior to having your students sort, give explicit directions and model a few examples.

Words for Sorting

pass	**gruff**
mess	grill
loss	stuff
kiss	stiff
tell	swell
bill	dress
spill	stress

Word ladders bring attention to sounds and letters as well as to word meanings.

Word Ladder: Make Jill the Boss

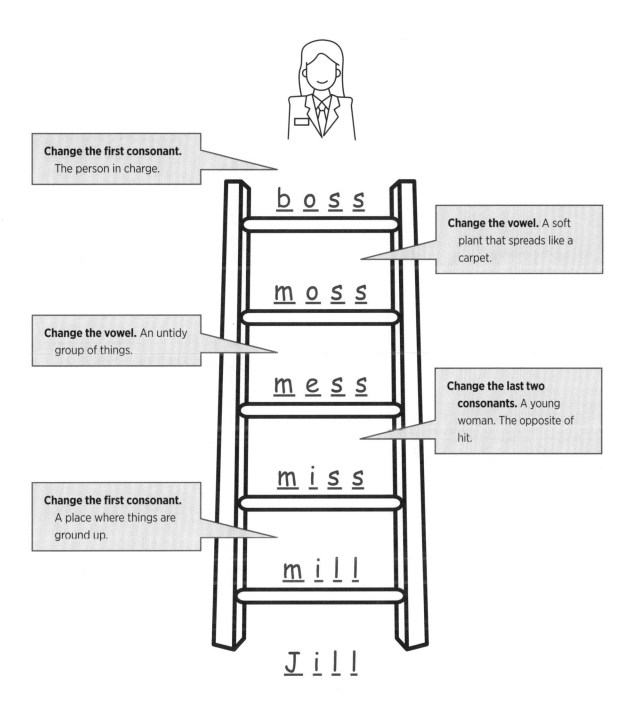

Change the first consonant. The person in charge.

b o s s

Change the vowel. A soft plant that spreads like a carpet.

m o s s

Change the vowel. An untidy group of things.

m e s s

Change the last two consonants. A young woman. The opposite of hit.

m i s s

Change the first consonant. A place where things are ground up.

m i l l

J i l l

Word Ladder: Huff and Puff up the Hill

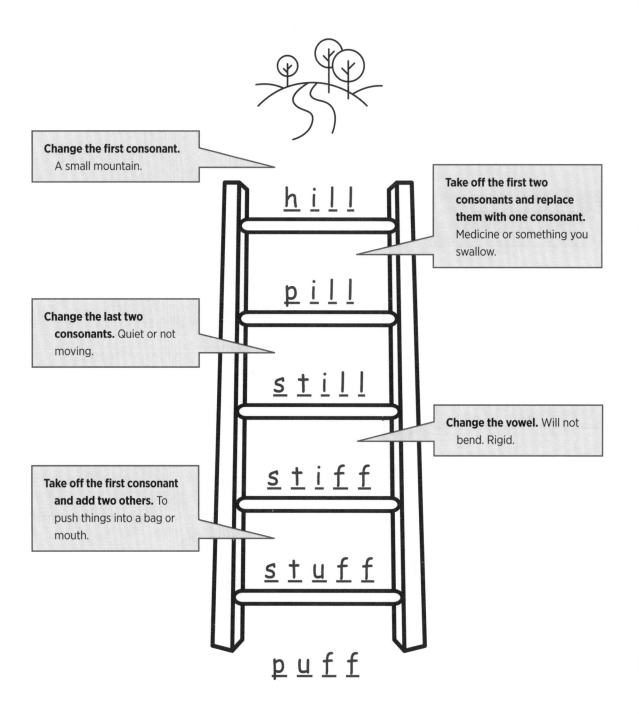

Change the first consonant. A small mountain.

Take off the first two consonants and replace them with one consonant. Medicine or something you swallow.

Change the last two consonants. Quiet or not moving.

Change the vowel. Will not bend. Rigid.

Take off the first consonant and add two others. To push things into a bag or mouth.

h i l l

p i l l

s t i l l

s t i f f

s t u f f

p u f f

Have students write with paper and pencil, whiteboard and marker, or electronic tablet.

Word Dictation

Suggested language for word dictation using the words *gruff* and *bluff* as examples appears below. For more practice, pull other words from the master spelling list.

Teacher: Get ready, everyone. The word is *gruff*. Say it with me.

Students and teacher: *Gruff.*

Teacher: You say it.

Students: *Gruff.*

Teacher: Listen: "I spoke in a *gruff* tone." *Gruff*. Write it.

Students: [As students write, teacher walks among them and scans for correct and incorrect words.]

Teacher: Listen and watch: "g-r-u-f-f, *gruff*." [Teacher writes word.] If your word is correct, give yourself a pat on the back. If it isn't correct, notice where you went wrong and correct it.

Teacher: Get ready for the next word. The word is *bluff*. Say it with me.

Students and teacher: *Bluff.*

Teacher: You say it.

Students: *Bluff.*

Teacher: If you can spell *gruff*, you can spell *bluff*. Write *bluff*.

Students: [They write.]

(Continue the process and language for any other dictation words you want to give.)

Always provide correct writing and spelling after each sentence.

Sentence Dictation

Sentences for dictation and reading

Do not spill the bag of chips.

I will kiss my mom.

I will not kiss the frog.

Did Bess dress up?

Kim will chop the bush and brush the moss.

Bill will huff and puff up the hill.

The man sat in the stiff grass.

My boss will hand me a box of cash.

I miss my lost stuff.

The man had to fill the bag with stuff.

Kim and Bess both had a red dress.

Suggested language for sentence dictation using *I miss my lost stuff* appears below.

Teacher: Get your whiteboards and markers ready for writing, everyone. The sentence is *I miss my lost stuff*. Say it with me.

Students and teacher: *I miss my lost stuff*.

Teacher: You say it.

Students: *I miss my lost stuff*.

Teacher: Write it.

Students: [As students write, teacher walks among them and scans for correct and incorrect words.]

Teacher: Listen and watch: "I miss my lost stuff." [Teacher writes sentence.] *Miss* and *stuff* each have a bonus letter at the end. If your words are spelled correctly, you started with a capital letter, and you have a correct ending mark, give yourself a pat on the back. If your sentence isn't correct, notice where you went wrong and fix it.

Post-Test

- At the end of your cycle of instruction, test your students by using the appropriate differentiated word list.

- Once you've effectively taught your students how to spell, not what to spell, you have the opportunity to add or substitute a word that isn't on the take-home list. For example, if *pill* was on the list, a student should also be able to spell *grill* or *still*.

- A post-test provides formative information. After giving the post-test, gather information about your students' needs and plan your next instructional steps. If students did not master the spelling features presented during this instructional cycle, consider reteaching the material in the upcoming cycle.

LESSON SET 4

Focus

- Two-syllable compound words

Points of Instruction

- Two one-syllable words can be put together to make a two-syllable word.
- Every syllable in this lesson has a short vowel sound.

> Review or reteach spelling concepts that have not yet been mastered. Some teachers teach children the term *digraph*. The letter combinations *ff*, *ll*, and *ss* are digraphs.

Additional Points to Review or Reteach

- A chant for short vowel sounds is "*a*, apple, /a/; *e*, Ed, /e/; *o*, octopus, /o/; *i*, itch /i/; *u*, umbrella /u/."
- A closed-syllable word has one vowel followed by one or more consonants. When the syllable's vowel is closed in by consonants, the vowel sound is short (with a few exceptions).
- Double letters or "bonus" letters occur at the end of one-syllable words that end in *f, s,* and *l*. Thus, the spellings for the sounds /f/, /l/, and /s/ at the end of one-syllable words are *ff, ll,* and *ss*.
- The spelling strategies "Use Sounds and Letters," "See the Word in Your Head," and "Spell by Analogy (Use a Word You Know)" can be used to spell these words.

Pre-Test

Use the pre-test in the following list to gather information about your students' needs, determine which differentiated list is appropriate for each student, and plan your next instructional steps.

The jaw drops twice for a two-syllable word. Vowels cause the jaw to drop.

Master Word List: two-syllable, closed syllable				Pre-Test List
catnap	upset	bobsled	pinball	hotshot
hotshot	sunlit	tomcat	uphill	lipstick
Batman	sunset	sunfish	upset	backpack
humbug	sunfish	gumdrop	nutshell	sunlit
lipstick	suntan	dishpan	gumball	bathtub
backpack	shotgun	dustpan		catfish
blacktop	gunshot	shellfish		gumdrop
crackpot	bathtub	zigzag		puffball
jackpot	catnip	pigpen		cobweb
chopsticks	catfish	puffball		uphill
		cobweb		

Don't worry if some word lists have more words than others. Give your students spelling lists based on what they need to learn, not on what others get.

Two Differentiated Word Lists	
List A	**List B**
catnap	humbug
hotshot	lipstick
Batman	backpack
humbug	dishpan
lipstick	shellfish
backpack	zigzag
cobweb	pigpen
tomcat	puffball
	gunshot
	nutshell
	uphill

You can give kids practice in more than one spelling strategy. Vary your Look Touch Say routine to touch upon multiple strategies.

Look Touch Say

Suggested language for practicing "Hear and Spell the Sounds"	
cobweb lipstick hotshot dishpan gunshot shellfish	**Teacher:** Look for a word with two /o/ sounds (short-*o*). Touch it. [Pause.] Say it. **Students:** *Hotshot.* **Teacher:** Look for a word with a /k/ sound. Touch it. [Pause.] Say it. **Students:** *Lipstick.* **Teacher:** How is the /k/ sound spelled in this word? **Students:** *C-k.* **Teacher:** Why is the /k/ sound spelled *c-k* in this word?

Suggested language for practicing "See the Word in Your Head"	
upset sunset suntan bathtub catnip catfish	**Teacher:** Look for *upset*. Touch it. [Pause.] Say it. **Students:** *Upset.* **Teacher:** See it. [They close their eyes.] Spell it. **Students:** *U-p-s-e-t.* **Teacher:** Look for *suntan*. Touch it. [Pause.] Say it. **Students:** *Suntan.* **Teacher:** See it. [They close their eyes.] Spell it. **Students:** *S-u-n-t-a-n.*

Look Touch Say Extension	
This Look Touch Say works for vocabulary (word meaning). It also incorporates "See the Word In Your Head."	
cane plan plane note slop backstroke inflate	**Teacher:** Look for the word that means tanned by the sun. Touch it. [Pause.] Say it. **Students:** *Suntan.* **Teacher:** Look for the word that is an antonym for happy or peaceful. Touch it. [Pause.] Say it. **Students:** *Upset.* **Teacher:** See it. [They close their eyes.] Spell it. **Students:** *U-p-s-e-t.*

By sorting, students learn how words are related. In this sort, there are numerous ways to relate words to each other. No guide words are given. When no specific categories are specified, the sort is an open sort.

Words for Sorting

crackpot	hotshot	oddball
cobweb	shellfish	puffball
unzip	undress	confess
lipstick	uphill	gumdrop
nutshell	humbug	backpack
dishpan	pigpen	zigzag

Do word ladder activities as a whole group until students learn the routine.

Word Ladder: Find a Jackpot in Your Backpack

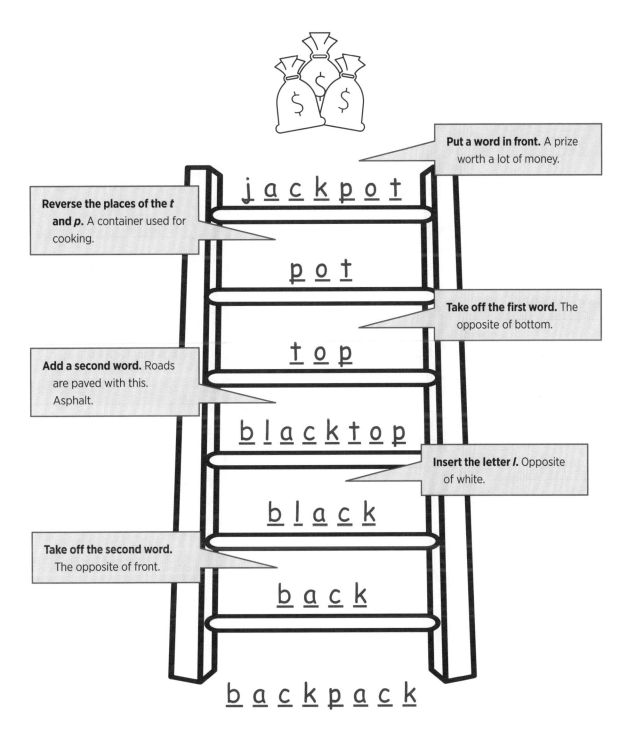

Put a word in front. A prize worth a lot of money.

j a c k p o t

Reverse the places of the _t_ and _p_. A container used for cooking.

p o t

Take off the first word. The opposite of bottom.

t o p

Add a second word. Roads are paved with this. Asphalt.

b l a c k t o p

Insert the letter _l_. Opposite of white.

b l a c k

Take off the second word. The opposite of front.

b a c k

b a c k p a c k

Word Ladder: Catnip for the Tomcat

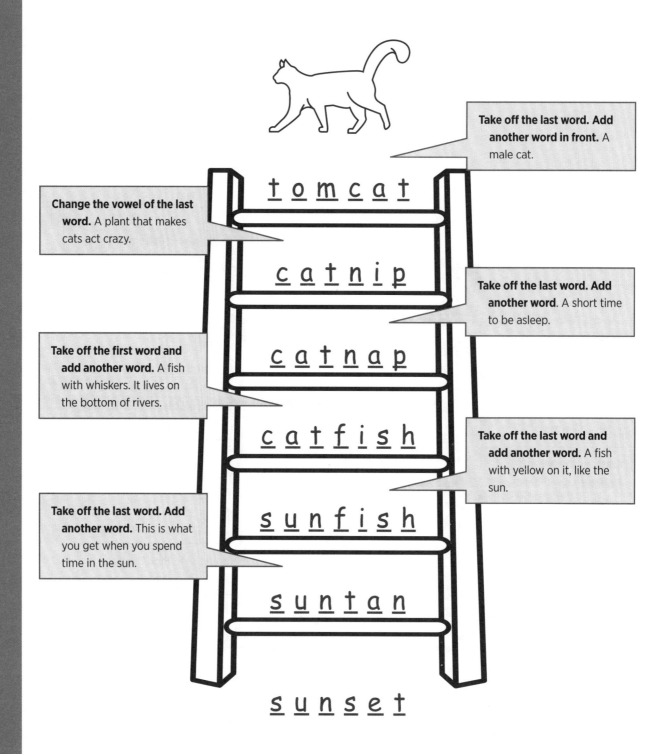

Take off the last word. Add **another word in front.** A male cat.

t o m c a t

Change the vowel of the last word. A plant that makes cats act crazy.

c a t n i p

Take off the last word. Add **another word**. A short time to be asleep.

c a t n a p

Take off the first word and add another word. A fish with whiskers. It lives on the bottom of rivers.

c a t f i s h

Take off the last word and **add another word.** A fish with yellow on it, like the sun.

s u n f i s h

Take off the last word. Add another word. This is what you get when you spend time in the sun.

s u n t a n

s u n s e t

More words for this activity can be found on this lesson set's master list.

Word Dictation

Suggested language for word dictation using the words *hotshot* and *catfish* as examples appears below. For additional practice, pull other words from the master spelling list.

> **Teacher:** Get ready, everyone. The word is *hotshot*. Say it with me.
>
> **Students and teacher:** *Hotshot.*
>
> **Teacher:** You say it.
>
> **Students:** *Hotshot.*
>
> **Teacher:** Put your hands under your chins and say it. [Students do this.] Write *hotshot*. Break it into syllables if you need to do that.
>
> **Students:** [As students write, teacher walks among them and scans for correct and incorrect words.]
>
> **Teacher:** Listen and watch: "h-o-t-s-h-o-t, *hotshot*." [Teacher writes word.] If your word is correct, give yourself a pat on the back. If it isn't correct, notice where you went wrong and correct it.
>
> **Teacher:** Get ready for the next word. The word is *catfish*. Say it with me.
>
> **Students and teacher:** *Catfish.*
>
> **Teacher:** You say it.
>
> **Students:** *Catfish.*
>
> **Teacher:** Write it.
>
> **Students:** [They write.]
>
> (Continue the process and language for any other dictation words you want to give.)

If a dictation sentence is too easy, choose a longer sentence with more complex words. Or make up your own sentence for dictation.

Sentence Dictation

Sentences for dictation and reading

I got a suntan.
Kim is a hotshot.
That catfish is big.
The puffball was small.
The pig was in the pigpen.
I can crack the nutshell.
Dad put the dish in the dishpan.
The dog in the bathtub was a mess.
Brad will dust the cobwebs in the den.
The loss upset Sid.

Suggested language for sentence dictation using *The puffball is small* appears below.

Teacher: Get your paper and pencils ready for writing, everyone. The sentence is *The puffball is small.* Say it with me.

Students and teacher: *The puffball is small.*

Teacher: You say it.

Students: *The puffball is small.*

Teacher: Write it.

Students: [As students write, teacher walks among them and scans for correct and incorrect words.]

Teacher: Listen and watch: "The puffball is small." [Teacher writes sentence.] *Puff, ball,* and *small* each have a bonus letter at the end. If your words are spelled correctly, you started with a capital letter, and you have a correct ending mark, give yourself a pat on the back. If your sentence isn't correct, notice where you went wrong and fix it.

Post-Test

- At the end of your cycle of instruction, test your students by using the appropriate differentiated word list.

- A post-test provides formative information. After giving the post-test, gather information about your students' needs and plan your next instructional steps. If students did not master the spelling features presented during this instructional cycle, consider reteaching the material in the upcoming cycle.

LESSON SET 5

Focus

- The long-*a* and long-*o* sounds spelled *a*-consonant-*e* and *o*-consonant-*e*

Points of Instruction

- This syllable type is called the vowel-consonant-*e* syllable.

- When a consonant and an *e* follow a vowel, that vowel sound is usually, but not always, long.

> **Whether you call it a magic *e* or say the *e* reaches over and pinches the vowel, engaging stories help children remember the vowel-consonant-e spelling.**

Additional Points to Review or Reteach

- Most words in our lists have one syllable. Our chins drop once when we say the word. Some words have two syllables. When we say these words, our chins drop twice.

- Some words in this lesson set have closed syllables, not vowel-consonant-*e* syllables. A closed-syllable word has one vowel followed by one or more consonants. When the syllable's vowel is closed in by consonants on the right, the vowel sound is typically short.

- The strategies "Use Sounds and Letters," "See the Word in Your Head," and "Spell by Analogy (Use a Word You Know)" can be used to spell words in this lesson set.

Pre-Test

Use the pre-test in the following list to gather information about your students' needs, determine which differentiated list is appropriate for each student, and plan your next instructional steps.

Asterisks denote phonograms on the thirty-seven high-frequency phonograms
list. Also, this list is categorized by closed and vowel-consonant-e syllables.

Master Word List: long-*a* and *o* (consonant-vowel-*e*) contrasted with short-*a* and *o*					Pre-Test List
an*, ap*, at*, am	*ake*, ape, ame*, ate*, ane*	*op*, ot, ob, ock**	*ope, oke*, ote, obe*	closed + VCe words	
can	cane	hop	hope	inflate	van
plan	plane	mop	mope	explode	tap
man	mane	slop	slope	backstroke	mane
van	vane	cop	rope	update	shape
cap	cape	not	note	cupcake	clock
tap	tape	clock	joke		broke
at	grape	block	broke		note
fat	shape	sock	woke		hope
hat	scrape	rob	choke		crop
rat	ate	glob	stroke		inflate
Sam	fate		robe		cupcake
	hate		globe		backstroke
	rate				
	same				
	cake				
	make				

Don't worry if some word lists have more words than others. Give your students
spelling lists based on what they need to learn, not on what others get.

Two Differentiated Word Lists	
List A	List B
can	trap
cane	scrap
plan	scrape
plane	block
crop	choke
slope	slope
clock	explode
joke	inflate
hat	backstroke
hate	

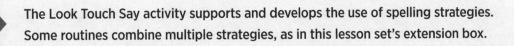

The Look Touch Say activity supports and develops the use of spelling strategies. Some routines combine multiple strategies, as in this lesson set's extension box.

Look Touch Say

Suggested language for practicing "Hear and Spell the Sounds"	
cane plan plane note slop backstroke inflate	**Teacher:** Look for a word with the /ane/ sound. Touch it. [Pause.] Say it. **Students:** *Cane/plane.* **Teacher:** Look for a word with the /ate/ sound. Touch it. [Pause.] Say it. **Students:** *Inflate.* **Teacher:** What sound do *cane, plane*, and *inflate* share? **Students:** /a/. **Teacher:** How do we spell the long-*a* sound in this lesson? **Students:** *A*-consonant-*e*.

Suggested language for practicing "Use a Word You Know"	
trap van mane grade joke code	**Teacher:** Look for a word with the *o*-consonant-*e* pattern. Touch it. [Pause.] Say it. **Students:** *Joke/code.* **Teacher:** If you said *joke* or *code*, you are correct! What pattern is shared by *joke* and *code*? **Students:** *O*-consonant-*e*. **Teacher:** If you can spell *joke*, you can spell *broke*. Tell your elbow buddy how to spell *broke*. [Children turn and spell.]

Look Touch Say Extension	
You can practice many strategies in one Look Touch Say routine. Here is suggested language for combining three strategies: "Think About Meaning," "Hear and Spell Sounds," and "See the Word in Your Head."	
cane plan plane note slop backstroke inflate	**Teacher:** Look for the word that means "put air into." Touch it. [Pause.] Say it. **Students:** *Inflate.* **Teacher:** Put your hand under your chin. Say *inflate*. [They say it.] How many syllables? **Students:** Two. **Teacher:** Say the first syllable and spell it. **Students:** *In. I-n.* **Teacher:** Say the second syllable and spell it. **Students:** *Flate. F-l-a-t-e.* **Teacher:** See the whole word in your head. [Students close eyes.] Number one students, tell a number two student how to spell *inflate*.

An open sort allows students to discover patterns on their own. Remove the bold printed words if they want to do an open sort.

Words for Sorting

can	**cane**	**hop**
hope	plan	plane
grape	strap	shave
inflate	explode	pack
broke	gap	tap
tape	backstroke	note
slop	rope	lame

A simple word ladder can toggle back and forth between the CVC pattern and the CVC*e* pattern—for example: *hate, hat, rat, rate, mate, mat, map, mop, hop, hope.*

Word Ladder: Rope a Hog

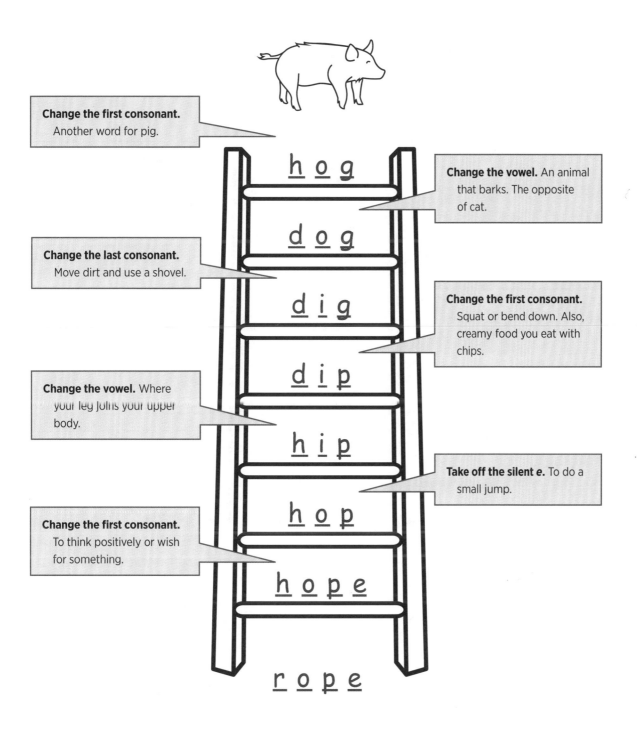

Change the first consonant. Another word for pig.

h o g

Change the vowel. An animal that barks. The opposite of cat.

d o g

Change the last consonant. Move dirt and use a shovel.

d i g

Change the first consonant. Squat or bend down. Also, creamy food you eat with chips.

d i p

Change the vowel. Where your leg joins your upper body.

h i p

Take off the silent *e*. To do a small jump.

h o p

Change the first consonant. To think positively or wish for something.

h o p e

r o p e

Word Ladder: Hop on a Plane

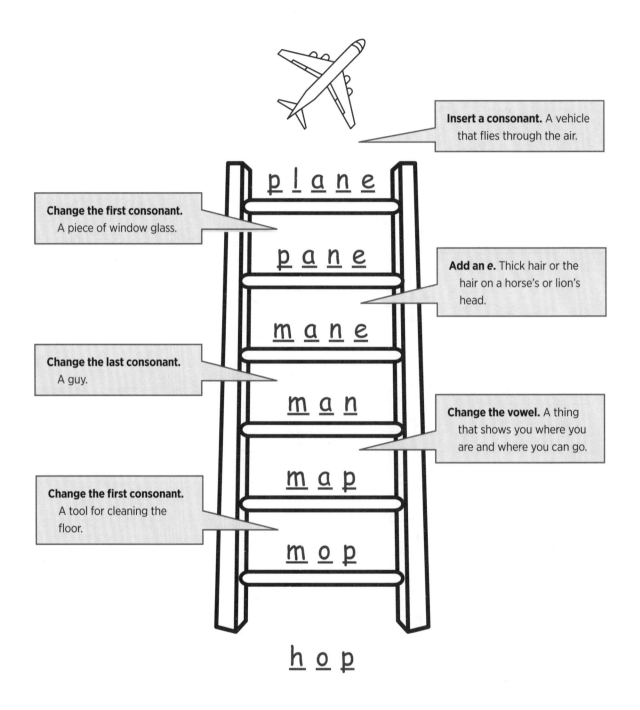

Have students write with paper and pencil, whiteboard and marker, or electronic tablet. Varying the medium keeps kids engaged week to week.

Word Dictation

Suggested language for word dictation using the words *hope* and *rope* as examples appears below. For additional practice, pull other words from the master spelling list.

Teacher: Get ready, everyone. The word is *hope*. Say it with me.

Students and teacher: *Hope*.

Teacher: You say it.

Students: *Hope*.

Teacher: Listen: "I *hope* it doesn't snow tomorrow." *Hope*. Write it.

Students: [As students write, teacher walks among them and scans for correct and incorrect words.]

Teacher: Listen and watch: "h-o-p-e, *hope*." [Teacher writes word.] If your word is correct, give yourself a pat on the back. If it isn't correct, notice where you went wrong and correct it.

Teacher: Get ready for the next word. The word is *rope*. Say it with me.

Students and teacher: *Rope*.

Teacher: You say it.

Students: *Rope*.

Teacher: If you can spell *hope*, you can spell *rope*. Spell *rope*.

Students: [They write.]

(Continue the process and language for any other dictation words you want to give.)

If the majority of your students struggle to remember the sentence after three times (I Say, We Say, You Say), it is fine to repeat the sentence one more time. Do what is right for your students.

Sentence Dictation

Sentences for dictation and reading

Kate left cake on her plate.

Bill and Kim had a late game.

Is there a snake in the grass?

Jane sent James a note.

Do not poke the snake and make it mad.

I had to rake the grass.

The dog had a black nose.

The plane will cross the lake.

The snake was like a black hose.

The cake had gumdrops on it.

If you inflate the ball, it may explode.

My dad made a bad joke.

Suggested language for sentence dictation using *The plane will cross the lake* appears below.

Teacher: Get your whiteboards and markers ready for writing, everyone. The sentence is *The plane will cross the lake*. Say it with me.

Students and teacher: *The plane will cross the lake.*

Teacher: You say it.

Students: *The plane will cross the lake.*

Teacher: Write it.

Students: [As students write, teacher walks among them and scans for correct and incorrect words.]

Teacher: Listen and watch: "The plane will cross the lake." [Teacher writes sentence.] If your words are spelled correctly, you started with a capital letter, and you have a correct ending mark, give yourself a pat on the back. If your sentence isn't correct, notice where you went wrong and fix it.

Post-Test

- At the end of your cycle of instruction, test your students by using the appropriate differentiated word list.

- Once you've effectively taught your students how to spell, not what to spell, you have the opportunity to add or substitute a word that isn't on the take-home list. For example, if *woke* was on the list, a student should also be able to spell *choke* or *stroke*.

- A post-test provides formative information. After giving the post-test, gather information about your students' needs and plan your next instructional steps. If students did not master the spelling features presented during this instructional cycle, consider reteaching the material in the upcoming cycle.

LESSON SET 6

Focus

- The long-*i* and long-*u* sounds spelled *i*-consonant-*e* and *u*-consonant-*e*

Points of Instruction

- When a consonant and an *e* follow a vowel, that vowel sound is usually, but not always, long.

> **Whether you call it a magic *e* or say the *e* reaches over and pinches the vowel, engaging stories help children remember the vowel-consonant-*e* spelling.**

Additional Points to Review or Reteach

- Most words in these lessons have one syllable. Our chins drop once when we say the word. When our chins drop twice, the word has two syllables.

- Vowel-consonant-*e* syllables are different from closed syllables. A closed syllable has one vowel followed by one or more consonants. When the syllable's vowel is closed in by a consonant, the vowel sound is short.

- The strategies "Use Sounds and Letters," "See the Word in Your Head," and "Spell by Analogy (Use a Word You Know)" can be used to spell these words.

- While engaged in other activities, such as teaching the routines of a spelling center or leading the building of words with letter tiles, remind students how the short and long vowel sound words compare with one another.

- Explicitly tell students that spelling centers and activities are opportunities for them to practice what they are learning in your lessons.

Pre-Test

Use the pre-test in the following list to gather information about your students' needs, determine which differentiated list is appropriate for each student, and plan your next instructional steps.

Pairing short vowel words with long vowel words (such as *pin/pine* and *cub/cube*) helps students understand the spelling of vowel-consonant-*e* words.

Asterisks denote phonograms on the thirty-seven high-frequency phonograms list.

Master Word List: long-*i* and *u* (consonant-vowel-*e*) contrasted with short-*i* and *u*					Pre-Test List
it*, in*, id, ick*	*ide, ife, ite*, ike, ine**	*ut, ub, uck**	*ute, ube, ule, une*	two-syllable VC*e* words	
in	pine	cut	cute	inside	pin
pin	fine	gut	flute	offside	slid
fin	mine	hut	brute	online	pine
tin	nine	nut	mute	lifelike	glide
did	shrine	cub	cube	lifetime	tub
hid	hide	tub	tube	compute	stuck
kid	pride	rub	rule		tube
rid	ride	duck	mule		flute
slid	slide	luck	dune		inside
bit	glide	muck	June		lifetime
lick	wide	puck	tune		compute
click	stride	stuck			
flick	bite	truck			
stick	life	struck			
	wife				
	bike				
	hike				

Consider giving your students a choice: Do they want their test to be on List A or List B?

Two Differentiated Word Lists	
List A	**List B**
pin	struck
slid	June
pine	slid
glide	shrine
tub	stride
luck	brute
stuck	mule
tube	inside
June	compute
	outside
	lifetime

The Look Touch Say activity supports and develops the use of spelling strategies such as "Spell by Analogy (Use a Word You Know)" and "Hear and Spell the Sounds."

Look Touch Say

Suggested language for "Spell by Analogy (Use a Word You Know)"	
pin slid pine glide tub luck stride	**Teacher:** Look for a word with the *i*-consonant-*e* pattern. Touch it. [Pause.] Say it. **Students:** *Pine/glide/stride.* **Teacher:** If you said *pine, glide,* or *stride,* you are correct. What pattern is shared by these words? **Students:** *I-consonant-e.* **Teacher:** If you can spell *glide,* you can spell *slide.* Tell your elbow buddy how to spell *slide.* [Children turn and spell.]

More practice with "Spell by Analogy (Use a Word You Know)"	
pin slid pine glide tub luck stride	**Teacher:** Look for a word with a short-*u* spelling. Touch it. [Pause.] Say it. **Students:** *Tub/luck.* **Teacher:** If you can spell *tub,* you can spell *grub.* Tell your elbow buddy how to spell *grub.* [Children turn and spell.]

Look Touch Say Extension	
You can practice more than one strategy in a Look Touch Say routine. Here is suggested language for combining "Think About the Meaning" with "Hear and Spell Sounds."	
pin slid pine glide tub luck lifetime compute	**Teacher:** Look for the word that means "move smoothly through the air." Touch it. [Pause.] Say it. **Students:** *Glide.* **Teacher:** Look for the word that means all the years that make up a life. Touch it. [Pause.] Say it. **Students:** *Lifetime.* **Teacher:** Put your hands under your chins. Say the word. [They say the word.] How many syllables? **Students:** Two. **Teacher:** Say the first syllable and spell it. **Students:** *Life. L-i-f-e.* **Teacher:** Say the second syllable and spell it. **Students:** *Time. T-i-m-e.* **Teacher:** See the whole word in your head. [Students close eyes.] A students tell B students how to spell *lifetime.*

Word sorts provide a great opportunity for students to *see* how spelling affects the sounds of letters in words.

Words for Sorting

pin	pine	tub
tube	rule	luck
truck	bit	bite
June	compute	inside
flute	nut	ride
rid	slide	shrine
offside	stuck	pride

Learning how short vowels are turned into long vowels through the addition of the silent *e* is a big step for students. Word ladders reinforce this learning. And for an effective and fun song that focuses on silent *e*, see Tom Lehrer's classic, "Silent E" (1972).

Word Ladder: Turn a Kid into a Cube

Add an e. A box, a three-dimensional shape.

c u b e

Change the vowel. A baby bear.

c u b

Change the first consonant. A car that takes you places.

c a b

Change the last consonant. A place to experiment.

l a b

Change the vowel. Run once around a track.

l a p

Change the last consonant. A part of a mouth.

l i p

Change the first consonant. The top of a box. A cover for a container.

l i d

k i d

Word Ladder: Turn a Nut into a Pine

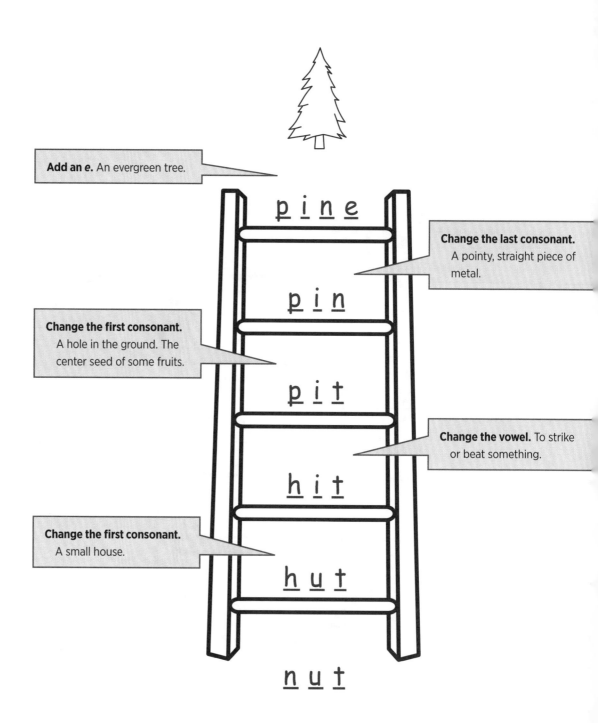

Add an e. An evergreen tree.

p i n e

Change the last consonant. A pointy, straight piece of metal.

p i n

Change the first consonant. A hole in the ground. The center seed of some fruits.

p i t

Change the vowel. To strike or beat something.

h i t

Change the first consonant. A small house.

h u t

n u t

The number of words you give to your students to practice depends upon the time you have to teach this activity and the needs of your students. More need means more practice.

Word Dictation

Suggested language for word dictation using the words *ride* and *slide* as examples appears below. For additional practice, pull other words from the master spelling list.

Teacher: Get ready, everyone. The word is *ride*. Say it with me.

Students and teacher: *Ride.*

Teacher: You say it.

Students: *Ride.*

Teacher: Listen: "I like to *ride* on my bike." *Ride.* Write it.

Students: [As students write, teacher walks among them and scans for correct and incorrect words.]

Teacher: Listen and watch: "r-i-d-e, *ride.*" [Teacher writes word.] If your word is correct, give yourself a pat on the back. If it isn't correct, notice where you went wrong and correct it.

Teacher: Get ready for the next word. The word is *slide*. Say it with me.

Students and teacher: *Slide.*

Teacher: You say it.

Students: *Slide.*

Teacher: If you can spell *ride*, you can spell *slide*. Spell *slide*.

Students: [They write.]

(Continue the process and language for any other dictation words you want to give.)

Find more words for sentences in this lesson set's master list.

Sentence Dictation

Sentences for dictation and reading

Kim Smith has a wide smile.

The bride had a fine time.

I will slide down the tube.

Jim will bite a stick of gum.

Rob brings a flute to band class.

A small cub is cute.

Use a cane if you limp.

I will ride my bike down the sand dune.

Your shrimp dish will win a prize.

The cat was cute, and the dog was a brute.

I like to ride my bike in June.

The stick stuck up from the mud.

Suggested language for sentence dictation using *I ride my fast bike in June* appears below.

Teacher: Get your whiteboards and markers ready for writing, everyone. The sentence is *I ride my fast bike in June.* Say it with me.

Students and teacher: *I ride my fast bike in June.*

Teacher: You say it.

Students: *I ride my fast bike in June.*

Teacher: Write it.

Students: [As students write, teacher walks among them and scans for correct and incorrect words.]

Teacher: Listen and watch: "I ride my fast bike in June." [Teacher writes sentence.] If your words are spelled correctly, you started with a capital letter, and you have a correct ending mark, give yourself a pat on the back. If your sentence isn't correct, notice where you went wrong and fix it.

Post-Test

- At the end of your cycle of instruction, test your students by using the appropriate differentiated word list.

- Once you've effectively taught your students how to spell, not what to spell, you have the opportunity to add or substitute a word that isn't on the take-home list. For example, if *cute* was on the list, a student should also be able to spell *mute* or *flute*.

- A post-test provides formative information. After giving the post-test, gather information about your students' needs and plan your next instructional steps. If students did not master the spelling features presented during this instructional cycle, consider reteaching the material in the upcoming cycle.

LESSON SET 7

Focus

- The /ar/, /or/, and /er/ sounds spelled *ar, or,* and *er*

Points of Instruction

- The *r* after the vowel changes the sound of the vowel.

> The vowel and consonant *r* are always presented together. There is no way to segment the primary short vowel sound and the *r* sound separately.

Additional Points to Review or Reteach

- Most words in our lists have one syllable. Our chins drop once when we say the word. When our chins drop twice, the word has two syllables.
- Some words on the list are compound. A compound word is made up of two words that can stand alone. For example, the word *popcorn* is made up of the words *pop* and *corn.*

Note

This lesson doesn't include suggested language for Look Touch Say, word dictation, or sentence dictation. If you have not previously used these three activities, please look to Lesson Sets 1–6 for language ideas. Use the words of your choice from this lesson's master spelling list to run the Look Touch Say and word-dictation activities. Sentences for dictation are given. Finally, Lesson Sets 7–10 contain only one ladder, unlike Lesson Sets 1–6, which contain two.

Pre-Test

Use the pre-test in the following list to gather information about your students' needs, determine which differentiated list is appropriate for each student, and plan your next instructional steps.

This syllable type is called the *r*-controlled syllable.

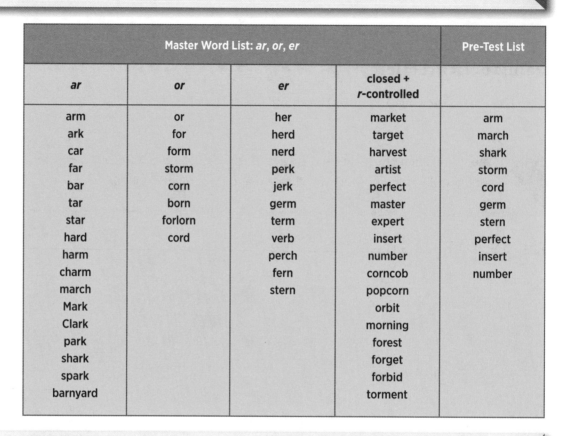

Master Word List: *ar, or, er*				Pre-Test List
ar	***or***	***er***	**closed +** **r-controlled**	
arm	or	her	market	arm
ark	for	herd	target	march
car	form	nerd	harvest	shark
far	storm	perk	artist	storm
bar	corn	jerk	perfect	cord
tar	born	germ	master	germ
star	forlorn	term	expert	stern
hard	cord	verb	insert	perfect
harm		perch	number	insert
charm		fern	corncob	number
march		stern	popcorn	
Mark			orbit	
Clark			morning	
park			forest	
shark			forget	
spark			forbid	
barnyard			torment	

This pattern shows the "bossy *r*." The *r* "bosses" the vowel into saying a different sound. Describing spelling features in terms of engaging stories helps students understand how words work.

Two Differentiated Word Lists	
List A	**List B**
arm	charm
car	march
form	shark
born	storm
hard	forlorn
march	cord
her	perch
verb	orbit
perch	concern
stern	perfect
popcorn	forbid
number	target

Words in bold can be "guide words" for a closed word sort. If you do an open sort, you can include the words in bold, or not.

Words for Sorting

arm	**for**	**her**
far	form	jerk
storm	start	germ
herd	cord	Mark
verb	shark	Ford
barnyard	corncob	expert
perfect	charming	morning

Create a short word ladder that toggles between the ar, or, and er spellings, such as *cord, card, hard, herd* and *port, part, cart, card, cord.*

Word Ladder: Turn Sharks into Ferns

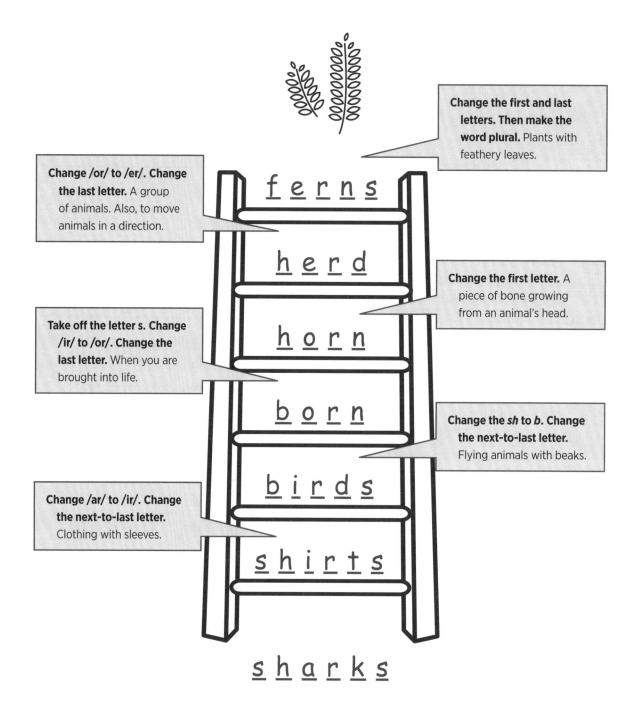

Change the first and last letters. Then make the word plural. Plants with feathery leaves.

Change /or/ to /er/. Change the last letter. A group of animals. Also, to move animals in a direction.

f e r n s

h e r d

Change the first letter. A piece of bone growing from an animal's head.

Take off the letter s. Change /ir/ to /or/. Change the last letter. When you are brought into life.

h o r n

b o r n

Change the *sh* to *b*. Change the next-to-last letter. Flying animals with beaks.

Change /ar/ to /ir/. Change the next-to-last letter. Clothing with sleeves.

b i r d s

s h i r t s

s h a r k s

> For word dictation, pull words from the master spelling list in this lesson set. Teacher language that can be used during word dictation is given in Lesson Sets 1–6.

> More words for making sentences can be found on this lesson set's master list.

Sentence Dictation

Sentences for dictation and reading

That shark bit my arm!

Mark was born in March.

The Ford truck was parked in the barnyard.

Kim looked forlorn.

Jane was concerned that she had germs.

Do not jerk the cord hard.

It was a perfect morning.

Her dad was a nerd and her mom was stern.

It is hard to harm a shark.

He drove his car into the storm.

Mark parked his car by a herd of sheep.

Do not get tar on the car.

He was a charming expert.

Post-Test

- At the end of your cycle of instruction, test your students by using the appropriate differentiated word list.

- Once you've effectively taught your students how to spell, not what to spell, you have the opportunity to add or substitute a word that isn't on the take-home list. For example, if *park* was on the list, a student should also be able to spell *shark* or *spark*.

- A post-test provides formative information. After giving the post-test, gather information about your students' needs and plan your next instructional steps. If students did not master the spelling features presented during this instructional cycle, consider reteaching the material in the upcoming cycle.

LESSON SET 8

Focus

- The /er/ sound spelled *or*, *ir*, and *ur*

Points of Instruction

- The *r* after the vowel changes the sound of the vowel. The vowel and the *r* go together and cannot be separated.
- This syllable type is called the *r*-controlled syllable. Some say the *r* "bosses" the vowel into saying a different sound.

> If you are not teaching syllable types (see "Introduction to the Lesson Sets" at the beginning of this chapter), don't worry about reviewing terms such as closed syllable.

Additional Points to Review or Reteach

- Many words in our lists have one syllable. Others have two.
- Some words are made from a closed syllable plus an *r*-controlled syllable.
- The strategies "Use Sounds and Letters," "See the Word in Your Head," and "Spell by Analogy (Use a Word You Know)" can be used to spell these words.

Note

This lesson doesn't include suggested language for Look Touch Say, word dictation, or sentence dictation. If you have not previously used these three activities, please look to Lesson Sets 1–6 for language ideas. Use the words of your choice from this lesson's master spelling list to run the Look Touch Say and word-dictation activities. Sentences for dictation are given. Finally, Lesson Sets 7–10 contain only one ladder, unlike Lesson Sets 1–6, which contain two.

Pre-Test

Use the pre-test in the following list to gather information about your students' needs, determine which differentiated list is appropriate for each student, and plan your next instructional steps.

> This lesson has three different spellings for the same sound. Conversely, one sound is spelled three different ways.

Master Word List: *or*, *ir*, *ur*				Pre-Test List
or	*ir*	*ur*	closed + *r*-controlled	
word	fir	fur	birdbath	actor
actor	stir	blur	chirping	doctor
tractor	girl	blurt	confirm	girl
doctor	bird	burn	songbird	shirt
mayor	dirt	churn	churning	church
color	flirt	church	slurping	slurp
armor	shirt	hurt	disturb	birdbath
	skirt	hurl	furnish	churning
	firm	curb		first
	birth	slurp		hurt
	chirp	surf		
	first	turf		
	third	murmur		
	swirl			
	twirl			

▶ You may wish to add or subtract words based on your students' capabilities.

Two Differentiated Word Lists	
List A	List B
bird	tractor
dirt	mayor
girl	color
first	first
actor	third
tractor	swirl
color	church
burn	murmur
church	disturb
hurt	churning
songbird	furnish
chirping	songbird

Word cards can also be used in the flip folder center.

Words for Sorting

actor	stir	fur
blur	third	word
tractor	churn	girl
doctor	shirt	blurt
firm	murmur	mayor
furnish	twirl	color
armor	disturb	birth

Do other activities, such as tumbling blocks and manipulating letter tiles, to teach how different words use different spellings of the /er/ sound.

Word Ladder: Bird Word

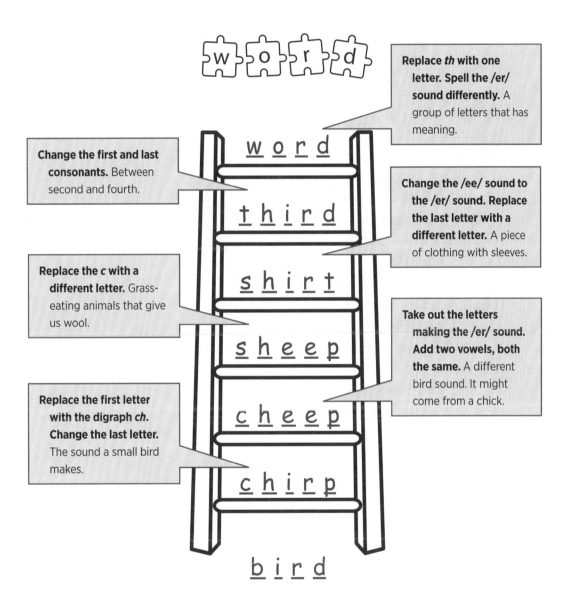

Replace *th* with one letter. Spell the /er/ sound differently. A group of letters that has meaning.

Change the first and last consonants. Between second and fourth.

Change the /ee/ sound to the /er/ sound. Replace the last letter with a different letter. A piece of clothing with sleeves.

Replace the *c* with a different letter. Grass-eating animals that give us wool.

Take out the letters making the /er/ sound. Add two vowels, both the same. A different bird sound. It might come from a chick.

Replace the first letter with the digraph *ch*. Change the last letter. The sound a small bird makes.

word

third

shirt

sheep

cheep

chirp

bird

Use these sentences for reading practice, too. Warm up by having students read a few decodable sentences you don't plan to dictate.

Sentence Dictation

Sentences for dictation and reading

Ben is a fine teacher and actor.

Kim saw the doctor for her burn.

Did you hear the songbird chirping?

Stop slurping your soup!

Jane is a girl in third grade.

The color of the tractor is green.

Stir the food so it does not burn.

Turf is dirt and grass.

Do not disturb me in church.

The armor was thick.

The twirling girl was a blur of color.

Did you wear a skirt or a shirt?

She gave birth to her first girl.

I can hurl the ball past the curb.

A doctor can help if you are hurt.

The dirty bird took a birdbath

Post-Test

- At the end of your cycle of instruction, test your students by using the appropriate differentiated word list.

- Once you've effectively taught your students how to spell, not what to spell, you have the opportunity to add or substitute a word that isn't on the take-home list. For example, if *actor* was on the list, a student should also be able to spell *factor* or *tractor*.

- A post-test provides formative information. After giving the post-test, gather information about your students' needs and plan your next instructional steps. If students did not master the spelling features presented during this instructional cycle, consider reteaching the material in the upcoming cycle.

LESSON SET 9

Focus

- The long-*a* sound spelled *ai* and *ay*; the /oi/ sound spelled *oi* and *oy*

Points of Instruction

- When the /a/ sound comes in the middle of a word (between consonants), as in *drain* and *paid*, the sound is often spelled *ai*. When the sound comes at the end of a word, as in *play* and *day*, it is often spelled *ay*.

- When the /oi/ sound comes in the middle of a word (between consonants), as in *coin* and *point*, the sound is spelled *oi*. When it comes at the end of a word, as in *boy* and *enjoy*, it is spelled *oy*.

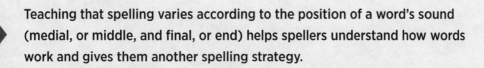

Teaching that spelling varies according to the position of a word's sound (medial, or middle, and final, or end) helps spellers understand how words work and gives them another spelling strategy.

Additional Points to Review or Reteach

- When the long-*a* sound is followed by a consonant, sometimes it is spelled *a*-consonant-*e*.

- Words that are pronounced the same way but spelled differently are called homophones. To correctly spell homophones, think about meaning. Some examples of homophones are *plane/plain, pane/pain, made/maid, male/mail, pale/pail,* and *mane/main*.

- The spelling strategies "Use Sounds and Letters," "See the Word in Your Head," "Think About Meaning," and "Spell by Analogy (Use a Word You Know)" can be used to spell these words.

Note

This lesson doesn't include suggested language for Look Touch Say, word dictation, or sentence dictation. If you have not previously used these three activities, please look to Lesson Sets 1–6 for language ideas. Use the words of your choice from this lesson's master spelling list to run the Look Touch Say and word-dictation activities. Sentences for dictation are given. Finally, Lesson Sets 7–10 contain only one ladder, unlike Lesson Sets 1–6, which contain two.

Pre-Test

Use the pre-test in the following list to gather information about your students' needs, determine which differentiated list is appropriate for each student, and plan your next instructional steps.

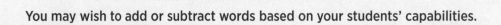

This syllable type is called a vowel-team syllable.

You may wish to add or subtract words based on your students' capabilities.

Master Word List: *ai*, *ay* (long-*a*), and *oi*, *oy*					Pre-Test List
ai	*ay*	*oi*	*oy*	syllable + vowel team	
aid	say	oil	boy	ashtray	rain
raid	May	boil	toy	playpen	paid
paid	pay	coil	joy	subway	train
braid	hay	foil	soy	staying	say
maid	day	spoil	toy box	archway	spray
tail	way	coin		daytime	foil
fail	pray	join		tinfoil	joint
snail	spray	joint		ointment	toy
mail	tray	moist		toilet	joy
rain	stray	oink		enjoy	playpen
main	payday	point		employ	tinfoil
brain	railway				
grain					
train					
strain					
sprain					
faint					
paint					
saint					
waist					
wait					
faith					

Two Differentiated Word Lists	
List A	List B
rain	sprain
train	braid
braid	faith
waist	stray
May	moist
tray	payday
wait	railway
rail	tinfoil
join	ointment
point	enjoy
spoil	subway
	employ
	daytime

Word sorts can help students see the medial and ending positions of the sounds. Students can sort these cards by sound or the position of the vowel team.

Words for Sorting

rain	say	oil
boy	raid	pray
spoil	joy	mail
tray	moist	toy
playpen	subway	tinfoil
ointment	point	railway
waist	enjoy	faint

Take the time to discuss the puns and figurative language presented in many of this book's word ladders.

Word Ladder: Foiled Again

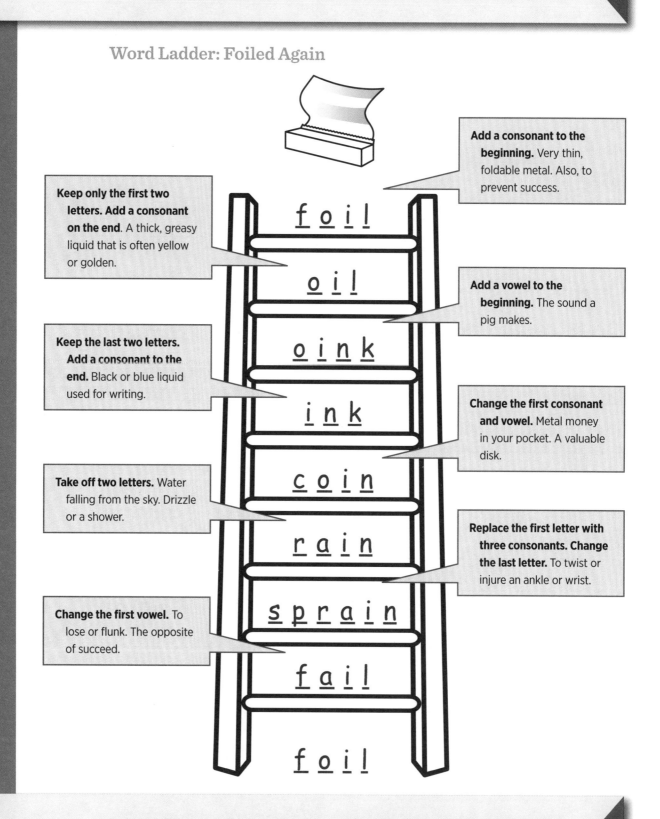

Add a consonant to the beginning. Very thin, foldable metal. Also, to prevent success.

f o i l

Keep only the first two letters. Add a consonant on the end. A thick, greasy liquid that is often yellow or golden.

o i l

Add a vowel to the beginning. The sound a pig makes.

o i n k

Keep the last two letters. Add a consonant to the end. Black or blue liquid used for writing.

i n k

Change the first consonant and vowel. Metal money in your pocket. A valuable disk.

c o i n

Take off two letters. Water falling from the sky. Drizzle or a shower.

r a i n

Replace the first letter with three consonants. Change the last letter. To twist or injure an ankle or wrist.

s p r a i n

Change the first vowel. To lose or flunk. The opposite of succeed.

f a i l

f o i l

For word dictation, pull words from the master spelling list in this lesson set. Teacher language that can be used during word dictation is given in Lesson Sets 1–6.

Spellers have to work hard to "see the words in their heads" and "think about the word's meaning," because sound does not always help us spell words correctly. (Consider, for example, *plain/plane, pain/pane, maid/made.*)

Sentence Dictation

Sentences for dictation and reading

Jane paid with five coins.

Kim rode the subway in the daytime.

Did the boy find a stray cat?

The train went down the main railway.

What is the point of a toy you do not enjoy?

I had to braid her hair.

A snail has a tail and a shell.

The maid will clean the playpen.

Did you oil the coil and flush the toilet?

Wrap the moist cake in tinfoil.

Did you enjoy the moist cake?

I pray it will rain today.

She made a clay ashtray.

The boy stayed away from the oinking pig.

The saint will paint the church.

In May, the rain will spray the cars.

Stay away from the boiling oil.

He put ointment on his sprained wrist.

Post-Test

- At the end of your cycle of instruction, test your students by using the appropriate differentiated word list.

- Once you've effectively taught your students how to spell, not what to spell, you have the opportunity to add or substitute a word that isn't on the take-home list. For example, if *nail* was on the list, a student should also be able to spell *snail* or *quail*.

- A post-test provides formative information. After giving the post-test, gather information about your students' needs and plan your next instructional steps. If students did not master the spelling features presented during this instructional cycle, consider reteaching the material in the upcoming cycle.

LESSON SET 10

Focus

- The long-*o* sound spelled *oa* and *ow*

Points of Instruction

- When the long-*o* sound comes in the middle of a word (between consonants), as in *boat* or *load*, the sound is often spelled *oa*.

- When the sound comes at the end of a word or syllable, as in *flow*, *grow*, and *shadow*, it is often spelled *ow*. The sound is also spelled *ow* when the word ends in *n*, as in *flown* and *grown*.

Teaching that spelling varies according to the position of a word's sound (medial, or middle, and final, or end) helps spellers understand how words work and gives them another spelling strategy.

Additional Points to Review or Reteach

- When the long-*o* sound is followed by a consonant, it is sometimes spelled *o*-consonant-*e*.

- Spellers have to work to "see the words in their heads" and "think about the word's meaning" because sometimes sound does not help us spell a word correctly. (Consider, for example, *load/lode*, *road/rode*, *groan/grown*.)

Note

- This lesson doesn't include suggested language for Look Touch Say, word dictation, or sentence dictation. If you have not previously used these three activities, please look to Lesson Sets 1–6 for language ideas. Use the words of your choice from this lesson's master spelling list to run the Look Touch Say and word-dictation activities. Sentences for dictation are given. Finally, Lesson Sets 7–10 contain only one ladder, unlike Lesson Sets 1–6, which contain two.

Pre-Test

Use the pre-test in the following list to gather information about your students' needs, determine which differentiated list is appropriate for each student, and plan your next instructional steps.

This syllable type is called a vowel team. In this lesson, the letter teams are also vowel digraphs. Two letters come together to make one sound. Even though *w* isn't traditionally considered a vowel, combinations such as *ew*, *ow*, and *aw* make a vowel team.

Master Word List: *oa, ow*			Pre-Test List
oa	*ow*	two-syllable vowel team	
oat	low	oatmeal	float
boat	mow	toaster	load
coat	row	moaning	grow
goat	blow	elbow	thrown
float	crow	window	soap
coach	flow	pillow	coast
coast	grow	yellow	know
roast	show	rainbow	toaster
toast	slow	shadow	shadow
croak	stow	swallow	
foam	tow	unknown	
moan	throw		
groan	know		
load	flown		
road	grown		
loaf	shown		
soap	thrown		
	known		

The *oa* and *ow* combinations are vowel digraphs. A diagraph consists of two letters that make one sound, such as *sh* or *ay*.

Two Differentiated Word Lists	
List A	List B
coat	coach
float	groan
low	flown
slow	thrown
know	toaster
coach	elbow
toast	swallow
yellow	window
shadow	unknown
oatmeal	grown
	rainbow

Word sorts can help students see the medial and ending positions of the sounds.

Words for Sorting

boat	**grow**	coach
coast	roast	groaning
moaning	slow	flow
throw	know	grown
thrown	flown	oatmeal
meatloaf	elbow	yellow
shadow	window	toaster

Word ladders are vehicles for exploring homophones, such as *groan/grown*, *moan/mown*, and *road/rowed*.

Word Ladder: The Snowy Goat

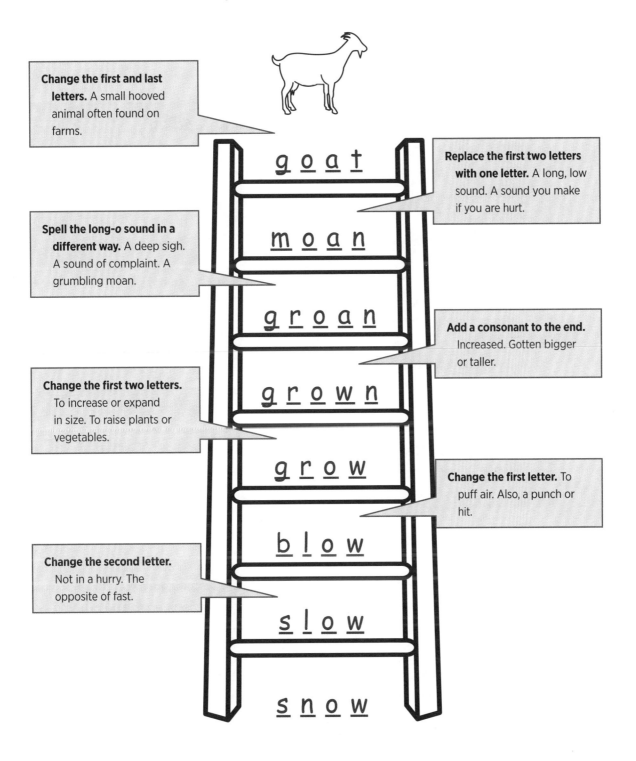

Change the first and last letters. A small hooved animal often found on farms.

g o a t

Replace the first two letters with one letter. A long, low sound. A sound you make if you are hurt.

m o a n

Spell the long-*o* sound in a different way. A deep sigh. A sound of complaint. A grumbling moan.

g r o a n

Add a consonant to the end. Increased. Gotten bigger or taller.

g r o w n

Change the first two letters. To increase or expand in size. To raise plants or vegetables.

g r o w

Change the first letter. To puff air. Also, a punch or hit.

b l o w

Change the second letter. Not in a hurry. The opposite of fast.

s l o w

s n o w

For teacher language to use during sentence dictation, see any lesson set 1–6.

Spellers have to work hard to "see the words in their heads" and "think about the word's meaning" because sound does not always help us spell words correctly. (Consider, for example, *no/know, toe/tow, groan/grown.*)

Sentence Dictation

Sentences for dictation and reading

Kate ate toast and oatmeal.

Bill and Kim floated a boat down the coast.

The man is moaning and groaning.

Kim did not want to swallow the burnt toast.

Jane does not know about the rainbow.

Do not throw toast to the goat.

I had to coach the kids.

We will load the car with yellow pillows.

Roast the meat and toast the bread loaf.

Did I grow a lot?

You have grown five inches!

Look out the window at the shadow.

The tow truck is big.

The frog can float and croak.

The number of times he has flown is unknown.

Post-Test

- At the end of your cycle of instruction, test your students by using the appropriate differentiated word list.

- Once you've effectively taught your students how to spell, not what to spell, you have the opportunity to add or substitute a word that isn't on the take-home list. For example, if *coast* was on the list, a student should also be able to spell *roast* or *toast.*

- A post-test provides formative information. After giving the post-test, gather information about your students' needs and plan your next instructional steps. If students did not master the spelling features presented during this instructional cycle, consider reteaching the material in the upcoming cycle.

CHAPTER 4

Lesson Sets for Teaching Spelling, Grade Band 3–5

LESSON SET 11

Focus

- The consonant-*le* syllable

Points of Instruction

- Consonant-*le* combines with a first syllable to make two-syllable words.

> Review or reteach any spelling concept that is not yet mastered. Below is a list of what you may want to review or reteach.

Additional Points to Review or Reteach

- The words in our lesson have two syllables. Your chin drops twice when you speak each word.
- The consonant-*le* spelling feature is a syllable type.
- The C-*le* syllable combines with other syllable types to form a two-syllable word. The other syllable types could be
  - a closed syllable (as in *gen-tle* or *sam-ple*),
  - an open syllable (as in *ti-tle* or *no-ble*),
  - a vowel-team syllable (as in *ea-gle* or *bee-tle*), or
  - an *r*-controlled syllable (as in *hur-dle* or *star-tle*).

- A closed syllable has one vowel followed by one or more consonants. There may be consonants before the vowel. When the syllable's vowel is "closed in" on the right by consonants, the vowel sound is short. Words or word parts such as *man, can, gen,* and *tram* are closed syllables.

- An open syllable has a vowel, and the vowel is *not* closed in by consonants on its right. There may be consonants before the vowel. When the syllable's vowel is "open," the vowel sound is long. Words or word parts such as *a, cra, no, he, i,* and *bu* are open syllables.

Pre-Test

Use the pre-test in the following list to gather information about your students' needs, determine which differentiated list is appropriate for each student, and plan your next instructional steps.

Every word in this lesson ends with a consonant-*le* syllable: *ble, cle, dle, gle, kle, ple,* and so on.

Master Word List: consonant-*le*			Pre-Test List
syllable + consonant-*le*	**closed syllable + consonant-*le***	**open syllable + consonant-*le***	
candle	crackle	able	candle
handle	buckle	cradle	bundle
bundle	chuckle	ladle	trample
mantle	freckle	maple	circle
gentle	pickle	staple	pickle
kindle	sprinkle	table	cradle
jungle	twinkle	cable	idle
jingle		fable	Bible
single		stable	bugle
tingle		idle	noble
trample		bridle	
gamble		Bible	
scramble		rifle	
mumble		title	
tumble		bugle	
circle		noble	
uncle			
sample			
simple			
purple			
startle			
turtle			

> You may wish to add or subtract words based on your students' capabilities.

Two Differentiated Word Lists	
List A	**List B**
candle	bundle
handle	gentle
uncle	trampling
circle	scramble
simple	circle
pickle	purple
sprinkle	chuckle
able	freckle
cable	cradle
maple	stapling
rifle	bugle
title	noble
	bridle

See Chapter 2 to review the strategies such as "Spell by Analogy (Use a Word You Know)" and "See the Word in Your Head."

Look Touch Say

Suggested language for practicing "See the Word in Your Head"	
pickle sprinkle able cable maple	**Teacher:** Look for *pickle*. Touch it. [Pause.] Say it. **Students:** *Pickle.* **Teacher:** See it. [They close their eyes.] Spell it. **Students:** *P-i-c-k-l-e.* **Teacher:** Look for *cable*. Touch it. [Pause.] Say it. **Students:** *Cable.* **Teacher:** See it. [They close their eyes.] Spell it. **Students:** *C-a-b-l-e.*

Suggested language for practicing "Spell by Analogy (Use a Word You Know)"	
purple buckle freckle cradle maple	**Teacher:** Look for a word with the *ckle* pattern. Touch it. [Pause.] Say it. **Students:** *Buckle/freckle.* **Teacher:** If you can spell *buckle*, you can spell *chuckle*. Tell your elbow buddy how to spell *chuckle*. [Students turn and spell.] **Teacher:** What do *maple*, *cradle*, *buckle*, and *freckle* have in common?

Look Touch Say Extension	
Sometimes students need to practice recognizing and reading words. Here is Look Touch Say language for practicing the skill of looking for and reading words.	
candle handle uncle circle simple	**Teacher:** Look for *handle*. Touch it. [Pause.] Say it. **Students:** *Handle.* **Teacher:** Look for *circle*. Touch it. [Pause.] Say it. **Students:** *Circle.* **Teacher:** Look for *candle*. Touch it. [Pause.] Say it. **Students:** *Candle.*

When working with sorts, students learn how words are related. Go beyond basic sorts to ones that look at different patterns, such as open versus closed first syllable or closed with no digraph (*gentle*) versus closed with digraph (*crackle*).

Words for Sorting

mantle	**hurtle**
table	staple
rifle	crackle
twinkle	sprinkle
buckle	tumble
startle	turtle
jingle	sparkle

Word ladders guide students to notice the sounds, letters, patterns, and meaning-making parts of words.

Word Ladder: A Light in the Jungle

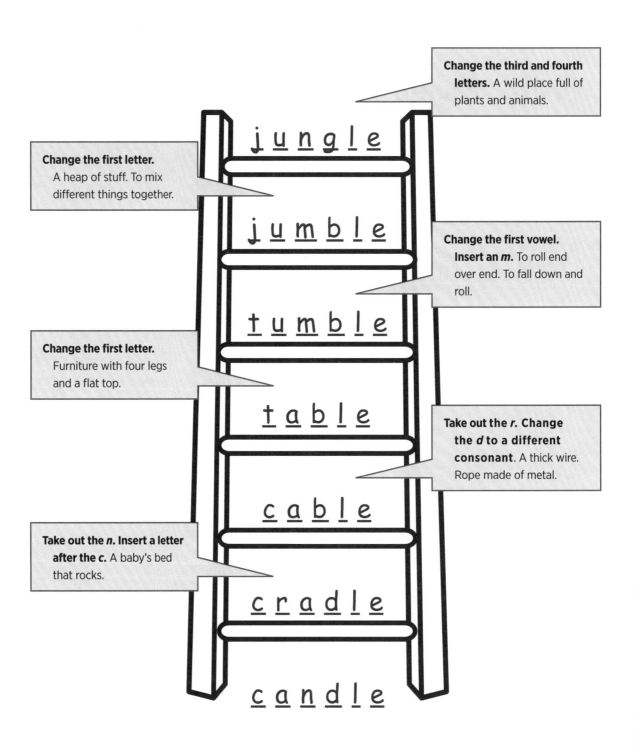

Change the third and fourth letters. A wild place full of plants and animals.

j u n g l e

Change the first letter. A heap of stuff. To mix different things together.

j u m b l e

Change the first vowel. Insert an *m*. To roll end over end. To fall down and roll.

t u m b l e

Change the first letter. Furniture with four legs and a flat top.

t a b l e

Take out the *r*. Change the *d* to a different consonant. A thick wire. Rope made of metal.

c a b l e

Take out the *n*. Insert a letter after the *c*. A baby's bed that rocks.

c r a d l e

c a n d l e

More words for this activity can be found in this lesson set's master list. Have students practice whatever words you think are appropriate.

Word Dictation

Suggested language for word dictation using the words *twinkle* and *sprinkle* as examples appears below. For additional practice, pull other words from the master spelling list.

S/D: Teacher: Get your whiteboards and markers ready for writing. The word is *twinkle*. Say it with me.

Students and teacher: *Twinkle*.

Teacher: You say it.

Students: *Twinkle*.

Teacher: Listen: "Stars *twinkle* in the night sky." Write *twinkle*.

Students: [As students write, teacher walks among them and scans for correct and incorrect words.]

Teacher: Listen and watch: "*t-w-i-n-k-l-e, twinkle*." [Teacher writes word.] If your word is correct, give yourself a pat on the back. If it isn't correct, notice where you went wrong and correct it.

Teacher: Get ready for the next word. The word is *sprinkle*. Say it with me.

Students and teacher: *Sprinkle*.

Teacher: You say it.

Students: *Sprinkle*.

Teacher: If you can spell *twinkle*, you can spell *sprinkle*. Spell *sprinkle*.

Students: [They write.]

(Continue the process and language for any other dictation words you want to give.)

Struggling readers can practice reading these decodable sentences as well as writing them. Pick the number of sentences based on the time you have and the needs of your students.

Sentence Dictation

Sentences for dictation and reading

What is the title of your story?

He kept the bridle in the stable.

One single turtle eats a green pickle.

Staple the paper to the table.

Put the Bible on the table by the rifle.

My uncle mumbles when he is mad.

Did you chuckle at his freckles?

He played his bugle by a maple tree.

His skin tingled as he tumbled down the steps.

The cost of cable will startle you.

She put sprinkles on her maple cupcake.

He cradled the ball and scrambled to the sideline.

A pickle in the jungle tastes really good.

Suggested language for sentence dictation using *The cost of cable will startle you* appears below.

Teacher: Get your whiteboards and markers ready for writing. The sentence is *The cost of cable will startle you.* Say it with me.

Students and teacher: *The cost of cable will startle you.*

Teacher: You say it.

Students: *The cost of cable will startle you.*

Teacher: Write it.

Students: [As students write, teacher walks among them and scans for correct and incorrect words.]

Teacher: Listen and watch: "The cost of cable will startle you." [Teacher writes sentence.] If your words are spelled correctly, you started with a capital letter, and you have a correct ending mark, give yourself a pat on the back. If your sentence isn't correct, fix it.

Post-Test

- At the end of your cycle of instruction, test your students by using the appropriate differentiated word list.

- Once you've effectively taught your students how to spell, not what to spell, you have the opportunity to add or substitute a word that isn't on the take-home list. For example, if *table* was on the list, a student should also be able to spell *cable* or *stable*.

- A post-test provides formative information. After giving the post-test, gather information about your students' needs and plan your next instructional steps.

LESSON SET 12

Focus

- The consonant-*le* syllable with a doubled consonant at the syllable juncture

Points of Instruction

- In many consonant-*le* words, the short vowel sound of the first syllable is maintained by doubling the consonant. The second consonant is there, but you don't hear it when you say the syllable. If the consonant were not there, however, the vowel sound would be long.

- Some words have a "vowel team" (vowel digraph), such as *ea* in *eagle* and *beagle* and *ee* in *beetle* and *needle*. The first syllable of many of these two-syllable consonant-*le* words has a long vowel sound. These words do not have a doubled consonant.

- When explaining the sound of a consonant-*le* ending, watch that you don't add a schwa sound to the consonant. For example, the pronunciation of the *ple* ending in *people* is a pure /p/ plus a pure /l/, not /puh/ plus /l/. The pronunciation of the syllable is /pl/ and not /puh-l/.

> The points below give ideas for reviewing or reteaching spelling concepts that have not yet been mastered.

Additional Points to Review or Reteach

- Every word in this lesson has two syllables. Your chin drops twice when you speak each word.

- The closed syllables that we hear when our chins drop, such as *ba* in *battle*, *fi* in *fiddle*, and *pu* in *puzzle,* are made closed by adding a consonant to them. We don't hear the consonant when we say the word, but we add it when we spell the word to make the vowel sound "short." The consonant is the same as the one that occurs in the consonant-*le* syllable. Thus, the middle consonant is doubled.

Pre-Test

- Use the pre-test in the following list to gather information about your students' needs, determine which differentiated list is appropriate for each student, and plan your next instructional steps.

> Every word in this lesson ends with a consonant-*le* syllable: *ble, cle, dle, gle, kle, ple,* and so on. The words with an asterisk have atypical vowel-team spellings.

Master Word List: consonant-*le*			Pre-Test List
closed syllable + consonant-*le*	closed syllable + consonant-*le*	vowel-team syllable + consonant-*le*	
battle	dribble	needle	battle
rattle	giggle	beetle	apple
cattle	fizzle	steeple	dribble
paddle	sizzle	noodle	giggle
saddle	wiggle	poodle	juggle
apple	jiggle	wheedle	needle
dazzle	bottle	eagle	poodle
waffle	gobble	beagle	eagle
pebble	cobble	people*	people
fiddle	nozzle	double*	trouble
middle	wobble	trouble*	
riddle	cuddle		
griddle	huddle		
little	muddle		
	bubble		
	juggle		
	puzzle		

It is fine that some students have more words to study than others. Differentiating gives students content that is right for them rather than content that is the same as everyone else's.

Two Differentiated Word Lists	
List A	List B
apple	paddle
pebble	giggle
little	dazzle
bottle	fiddle
bubble	huddle
puzzle	nozzle
middle	eagle
needle	poodle
people	steeple
trouble	people
	double
	trouble

Choose the Look Touch Say box that has language matching what you want to teach.

Look Touch Say

Suggested language for practicing "Spell by Analogy (Use a Word You Know)"	
puzzle middle needle beetle people double	**Teacher:** Look for a word with the doubled consonant pattern. Touch it. [Pause.] Say it. **Students:** *Puzzle/middle.* **Teacher:** If you can spell *middle*, you can spell *griddle*. Tell your elbow buddy how to spell *griddle*. [Children turn and spell.] **Teacher:** Why do *puzzle, middle, and griddle* have doubled consonants in the middle?

Suggested language for practicing "See the Word in Your Head"	
apple pebble little bottle bubble	**Teacher:** Look for *little.* Touch it. [Pause.] Say it. **Students:** Little. **Teacher:** See it. [They close their eyes.] Spell it. **Students:** *L-i-t-t-l-e.* **Teacher:** Look for *bubble.* Touch it. [Pause.] Say it. **Students:** *Bubble.* **Teacher:** See it. [They close their eyes.] Spell it. **Students:** *B-u-b-b-l-e.*

Look Touch Say Extension	
This Look Touch Say is a way to practice vocabulary (word meaning). It also incorporates "See the Word in Your Head."	
puzzle middle needle beetle people double	**Teacher:** Look for the word that is a type of insect with a hard back. Touch it. [Pause.] Say it. **Students:** *Beetle.* **Teacher:** Look for the word that means a point that is the same distance from the beginning and end. Touch it. [Pause.] Say it. **Students:** *Middle.* **Teacher:** See it. [They close their eyes.] Spell it. **Students:** *M-i-d-d-l-e.*

Words in bold can be "guide words" for a closed word sort. The word *people* sorts loosely with *needle* or *double*. So does the word *trouble*. When monitoring sorts, ask students, "Why did you put these words together?"

Words for Sorting

battle	**needle**
double	dribble
wiggle	gobble
people	middle
trouble	pebble
waffle	rattle
riddle	beetle

Do word ladder activities as a whole group until students learn the routine.

Word Ladder: Battle an Eagle

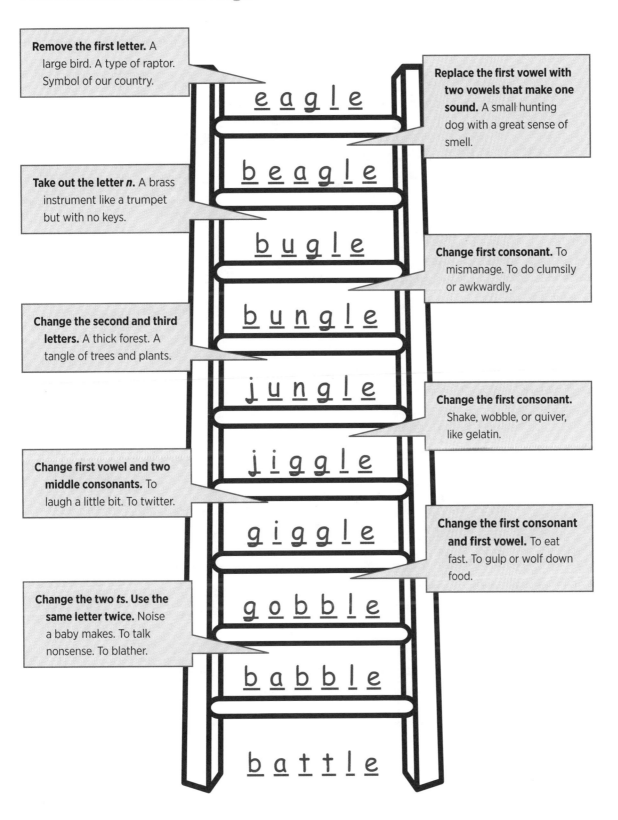

Remove the first letter. A large bird. A type of raptor. Symbol of our country.

Replace the first vowel with two vowels that make one sound. A small hunting dog with a great sense of smell.

Take out the letter *n*. A brass instrument like a trumpet but with no keys.

Change first consonant. To mismanage. To do clumsily or awkwardly.

Change the second and third letters. A thick forest. A tangle of trees and plants.

Change the first consonant. Shake, wobble, or quiver, like gelatin.

Change first vowel and two middle consonants. To laugh a little bit. To twitter.

Change the first consonant and first vowel. To eat fast. To gulp or wolf down food.

Change the two *ts*. Use the same letter twice. Noise a baby makes. To talk nonsense. To blather.

eagle

beagle

bugle

bungle

jungle

jiggle

giggle

gobble

babble

battle

Set aside four or five minutes once or twice a week to do word dictation.

Word Dictation

Suggested language for word dictation using the words *giggle* and *wiggle* as examples appears below. For additional practice, pull other words from the master spelling list.

Teacher: Get your whiteboards and markers ready for writing, everyone. The word is *giggle*. Say it with me.

Students and teacher: *Giggle.*

Teacher: You say it.

Students: *Giggle.*

Teacher: Listen: "The baby began to *giggle*." Write *giggle*.

Students: [As students write, teacher walks among them and scans for correct and incorrect words.]

Teacher: Listen and watch: "*G-i-g-g-l-e, giggle*." [Teacher writes word.] If your word is correct, give yourself a pat on the back. If it isn't correct, notice where you went wrong and correct it.

Teacher: Get ready for the next word. The word is *wiggle*. Say it with me.

Students and teacher: *Wiggle.*

Teacher: You say it.

Students: *Wiggle.*

Teacher: If you can spell *giggle*, you can spell *wiggle*. Spell *wiggle*.

Students: [They write.]

(Continue the process and language for any other dictation words you want to give.)

In the sentences, you don't have to use words found on the students' take-home spelling lists. Use words from the master spelling list.

Sentence Dictation

Sentences for dictation and reading

The little girl began to giggle.

Pass me a waffle and an apple.

The baby has a bottle and a rattle.

The people huddled in the middle of the sidewalk.

I saw a beetle by the pebble.

Can a poodle gobble noodles?

Can you blow bubbles or juggle apples?

If you wiggle and giggle in church, you will get in trouble.

The puzzle was a lot of trouble.

An eagle and a beagle battled for a noodle.

Jiggle the handle to open the door.

I can play a little fiddle and gobble lots of waffles.

The steeple was as pointy as a needle.

Suggested language for sentence dictation using *The poodle gobbled oodles of noodles* appears below.

Teacher: Get your whiteboards and markers ready for writing, everyone. The sentence is *The poodle gobbled oodles of noodles.* Say it with me.

Students and teacher: *The poodle gobbled oodles of noodles.*

Teacher: You say it.

Students: *The poodle gobbled oodles of noodles.*

Teacher: Write it.

Students: [As students write, teacher walks among them and scans for correct and incorrect words.]

Teacher: Listen and watch: *The poodle gobbled oodles of noodles.* [Teacher writes sentence.] If your words are spelled correctly, you started with a capital letter, and you have a correct ending mark, give yourself a pat on the back. If your sentence isn't correct, fix it.

Post-Test

- At the end of your cycle of instruction, test your students by using the appropriate differentiated word list.

- Once you've effectively taught your students how to spell, not what to spell, you have the opportunity to add or substitute a word that isn't on the take-home list. For example, if *middle* was on the list, a student should also be able to spell *fiddle* or *riddle*.

- A post-test provides formative information. After giving the post-test, gather information about your students' needs and plan your next instructional steps.

LESSON SET 13

Focus

- Multisyllabic words formed with suffixes *ion* and *ive*

Points of Instruction

- Suffixes add meaning to words.

- The *ion* suffix forms a noun. It means "act of, state of, or result of." It can be in one of two forms: *tion* or *sion*.

- When the *sion* is against an open syllable, as in *fusion* and *invasion*, the sound of the s is /zh/ rather than /sh/. When it is against a closed syllable, as in *admission* and *extension*, its sound is /sh/.

- The *ive* suffix forms an adjective. It means "toward an action" or "tending toward the act of." It is often spelled with a *t*, as in *tive*, or an *s*, as in *sive*.

- The *ion* and *ive* suffixes can be combined with other syllables to form multisyllabic nouns and adjectives. More specifically, they can be combined with closed, open, vowel-team, and *r*-controlled syllables.

If you are not teaching students about the syllable types, then omit references to closed syllables, open syllables, and so on.

Additional Points to Review or Reteach

- The words in our lesson have multiple syllables. Your chin drops two or more times when you speak each word.

- Open syllables contain a vowel that is *not* closed in by a consonant to its right. The sound of the vowel is typically long. Sometimes the vowel sound is the schwa sound, which is most frequently pronounced as the short-*u* sound (as in *cup*) and occurs in unaccented syllables. You can hear the /u/ sound in the first and last *a* of *Alaska*, the *i* in *family*, and the *o* in *parrot*. Perhaps the easiest schwa sound to recognize is /u/ sound, made by the letter *e* in the word *the*.

Pre-Test

Use the pre-test in the following list to gather information about your students' needs, determine which differentiated list is appropriate for each student, and plan your next instructional steps.

Each word column is further divided by syllable types. For example, in the *tion* column, words are grouped by closed syllables + *tion*, then open syllables + *tion*, then multiple syllable types.

This lesson set is the first one to include three differentiated words lists. Three lists give you the ability to more fully meet the needs of a greater variety of students.

Master Word List: *ion* and *ive* suffixes				Pre-Test List
tion	*sion*	*tive*	*sive*	
action	mission	active	massive	action
fraction	session	inactive	cursive	option
option	percussion	captive	expensive	invention
section	concussion	negative	exclusive	exploration
caption	admission	positive	offensive	mission
fiction	expression	primitive	defensive	expression
question	permission	sensitive	expansive	confusion
objection	extension	native	inventive	active
subtraction	vision	creative		primitive
invention	television	fugitive		native
station	fusion	elective		defective
nation	confusion	effective		
motion	explosion	defective		
notion	division	addictive		
lotion	invasion			
rotation	inclusion			
vacation	dimension			
pollution				
reaction				
inflation				
creation				
position				
exploration				
evaporation				
multiplication				

Three Differentiated Word Lists		
List A	**List B**	**List C**
action	invention	objection
option	question	invention
fiction	nation	subtraction
nation	station	exploration
station	inflation	evaporation
lotion	admission	percussion
vision	expression	concussion
fusion	vision	invasion
active	explosion	dimension
captive	positive	primitive
native	negative	fugitive
massive	cursive	exclusive
cursive	expensive	defensive

Children (and adults) sometimes use words they know to read words they don't know. The same strategy can be applied in spelling.

Look Touch Say

Suggested language for practicing "See the Word in Your Head"	
action option fiction nation station lotion	**Teacher:** Look for *action*. Touch it. [Pause.] Say it. **Students:** *Action.* **Teacher:** See it. [They close their eyes.] Spell it. **Students:** *A-c-t-i-o-n.* **Teacher:** Look for *nation*. Touch it. [Pause.] Say it. **Students:** *Nation.* **Teacher:** See it. [They close their eyes.] Spell it. **Students:** *N-a-t-i-o-n.*

Suggested language for practicing "Spell by Analogy (Use a Word You Know)"	
inflation mission expression vision explosion	**Teacher:** Look for a word with the double-*s* pattern. Touch it. [Pause.] Say it. **Students:** *Mission/ expression.* **Teacher:** If you said *mission* or *expression*, you are correct. What pattern is shared with these two words? **Students:** Double *s.* **Teacher:** If you can spell *mission*, you can spell *admission*. Tell your elbow buddy how to spell *admission*. [Students turn and spell.]

Look Touch Say Extension	
Sometimes students need to practice recognizing and reading words. Here is Look Touch Say language for practicing the skill of looking for and reading words.	
action fiction nation station lotion	**Teacher:** Look for *fiction*. Touch it. [Pause.] Say it. **Students:** *Fiction.* **Teacher:** Look for *station*. Touch it. [Pause.] Say it. **Students:** *Station.* **Teacher:** Look for *action*. Touch it. [Pause.] Say it. **Students:** *Action.*

Through sorts, students notice similarities and differences between words.

Words for Sorting

action	**nation**
mission	**captive**
section	question
rotation	vacation
primitive	sensitive
extension	vision
percussion	creative

Spelling and vocabulary meaning come together in a word ladder.

Word Ladder: Don't Be a Couch Potato

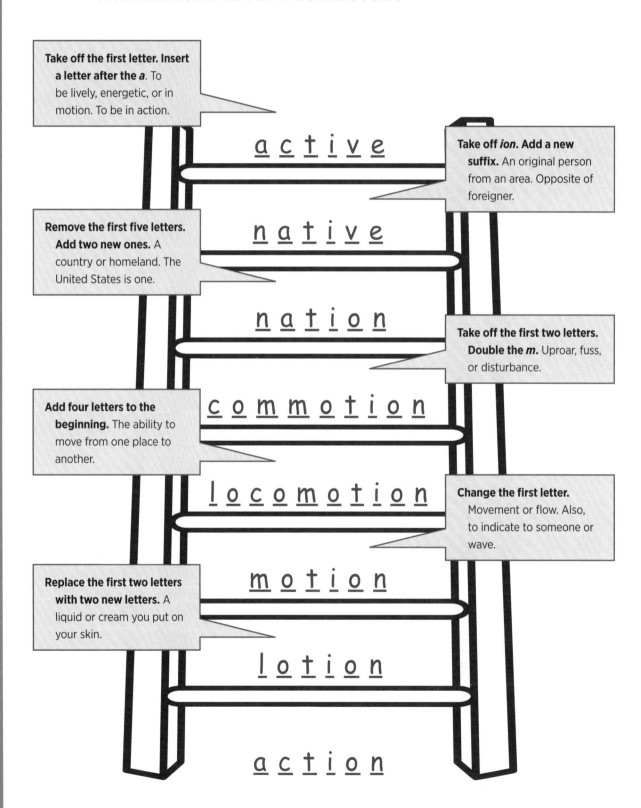

Take off the first letter. Insert a letter after the *a*. To be lively, energetic, or in motion. To be in action.

active

Take off *ion*. Add a new suffix. An original person from an area. Opposite of foreigner.

Remove the first five letters. Add two new ones. A country or homeland. The United States is one.

native

nation

Take off the first two letters. Double the *m*. Uproar, fuss, or disturbance.

Add four letters to the beginning. The ability to move from one place to another.

commotion

locomotion

Change the first letter. Movement or flow. Also, to indicate to someone or wave.

Replace the first two letters with two new letters. A liquid or cream you put on your skin.

motion

lotion

action

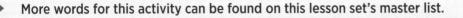

More words for this activity can be found on this lesson set's master list.

Word Dictation

Suggested language for word dictation using the words *question* and *confusion* as examples appears below. For additional practice, pull other words from the master spelling list.

Teacher: Get your whiteboards and markers ready for writing, everyone. The word is *question*. Say it with me.

Students and teacher: *Question.*

Teacher: You say it.

Students: *Question.*

Teacher: Listen: "I will ask you a *question*." Write *question*.

Students: [As students write, teacher walks among them and scans for correct and incorrect words.]

Teacher: Listen and watch: "*Q-u-e-s-t-i-o-n, question*." [Teacher writes word.] If your word is correct, give yourself a pat on the back. If it isn't correct, notice where you went wrong and correct it.

Teacher: Get ready for the next word. The word is *confusion*. Say it with me.

Students and teacher: *Confusion.*

Teacher: You say it.

Students: *Confusion.*

Teacher: If you can spell *fusion*, you can spell *confusion*. Spell *confusion*.

Students: [They write.]

(Continue the process and language for any other dictation words you want to give.)

If a dictation sentence is too easy, choose a longer sentence with more complex words. Or pick two sentences—one shorter and one longer—and give students the option to choose the one they want.

Sentence Dictation

Sentences for dictation and reading

The percussion section played with expression.

You have an option to do addition or subtraction.

He is a sensitive and creative person.

Are you positive they are on vacation?

You have my permission to practice cursive writing.

My invention gets rid of massive pollution.

An invasion is offensive, not defensive.

There was an explosion at the station.

Can you stay in motion if you have a concussion?

The television screen was defective.

Your cursive writing is expansive and inventive.

Once a captive, the fugitive was now on the loose.

Suggested language for sentence dictation using *There was an explosion at the station* appears below.

Teacher: Get your electronic tablets ready for writing, everyone. The sentence is *There was an explosion at the station.* Say it with me.

Students and teacher: *There was an explosion at the station.*

Teacher: You say it.

Students: *There was an explosion at the station.*

Teacher: Write it.

Students: [As students write, teacher walks among them and scans for correct and incorrect words.]

Teacher: Listen and watch: *"There was an explosion at the station."* [Teacher writes sentence.] If your words are spelled correctly, you started with a capital letter, and you have a correct ending mark, give yourself a pat on the back. If your sentence isn't correct, fix it.

Post-Test

- At the end of your cycle of instruction, test your students using the appropriate differentiated word list.

- Once you've effectively taught your students how to spell, not what to spell, you have the opportunity to add or substitute a word that isn't on the take-home list. For example, if *action* was on the list, a student should also be able to spell *fraction* or *traction*.

- A post-test provides formative information. After giving the post-test, gather information about your students' needs and plan your next instructional steps.

LESSON SET 14

Focus

- Multisyllabic words with the suffix *er*, *or*, and *en*

Points of Instruction

- The *er* and *or* suffixes mean "one who" or "a thing that," as a *teacher* is one who teaches and a *radiator* is a thing that radiates.
- The *en* suffix means "made from" (as *wooden* means "made from wood") or "to make" (as *tighten* means "to make tight").

> Reviewing and reteaching takes time, but it is necessary for students who have not yet mastered a skill. Centers, more complex words, and variations within activities enable you to differentiate (while you reteach), thus keeping students who have mastered the skills on track, too.

Additional Points to Review or Reteach

- Suffixes add meaning to words.
- The jaw drops multiple times for a multisyllabic word, once for each vowel sound.
- The syllables that make up the words in this lesson's master list are closed, open, vowel team, and *r*-controlled.
- The strategies "See the Word in Your Head," "Spell by Analogy (Use a Word You Know)," and "Think About Meaning" can be used to spell these words.

Pre-Test

Use the pre-test in the following list to gather information about your students' needs, determine which differentiated list is appropriate for each student, and plan your next instructional steps.

> Take some time to discuss what the base words are. Then show how a suffix changes the meaning of the base words. Note that the *en* list is divided into adjectives (for example, *oaken*) and verbs (for example, *tighten*).

Master Word List: *er*, *or*, and *en* suffix			Pre-Test List
***er* suffix**	***or* suffix**	***en* suffix**	
player	actor	oaken	thinker
banker	doctor	silken	trader
farmer	victor	wooden	provider
hunter	captor	ashen	sponsor
thinker	raptor	woolen	neighbor
baker	sponsor	golden	detector
maker	donor	dampen	oaken
trader	tutor	sicken	loosen
teacher	tailor	fasten	awaken
preacher	jailor	soften	stolen
pitcher	sailor	harden	
catcher	author	darken	
loser	savior	tighten	
winner	neighbor	fallen	
shopper	editor	stolen	
gangster	creator	broken	
fighter	senator	deepen	
provider	conductor	loosen	
producer	director	awaken	
	predator	whiten	
	governor	fatten	
	operator	sunken	
	radiator		

If three lists are too difficult to manage, consider running two lists. Conversely, if you've been running two lists, consider giving three.

Three Differentiated Word Lists		
List A	**List B**	**List C**
player	preacher	preacher
banker	pitcher	pitcher
thinker	catcher	provider
baker	gangster	producer
teacher	fighter	savior
actor	neighbor	neighbor
doctor	doctor	predator
sponsor	creator	governor
sailor	senator	operator
neighbor	conductor	superior
wooden	director	radiator
golden	woolen	woolen
sicken	golden	golden

> The Look Touch Say activity supports and develops the use of spelling strategies.

Look Touch Say

Suggested language for practicing "See the Word in Your Head"	
shopper gangster fighter neighbor	**Teacher:** Look for *fighter*. Touch it. [Pause.] Say it. **Students:** *Fighter*. **Teacher:** See it. [They close their eyes.] Spell it out loud. **Students:** *F-i-g-h-t-e-r*. **Teacher:** Look for *neighbor*. Touch it. [Pause.] Say it. **Students:** *Neighbor*. **Teacher:** See it. [They close their eyes.] Spell it in writing. [They open their eyes and write the word.]

Suggested language for practicing "Spell by Analogy (Use a Word You Know)"	
trader teacher actor doctor wooden golden	**Teacher:** Look for a word that ends with the suffix *or*. Touch it. [Pause.] Say it. **Students:** *Actor/doctor*. **Teacher:** Look for a word that ends with the suffix *en*. Touch it. [Pause.] Say it. **Students:** *Wooden/golden*. **Teacher:** What do all of these words end with? **Students:** A suffix.

Look Touch Say Extension	
This Look Touch Say is a way to practice vocabulary (word meaning). It also incorporates "See the Word in Your Head."	
creator senator conductor director woolen golden	**Teacher:** Look for the word that means "one who conducts or a thing that conducts." Touch it. [Pause.] Say it. **Students:** *Conductor*. **Teacher:** Look for the word that means the opposite of "one who destroys." Touch it. [Pause.] Say it. **Students:** *Creator*. **Teacher:** See it. [They close their eyes.] Spell it. **Students:** *C-r-e-a-t-o-r*.

An open sort allows students to find patterns on their own while constructing meaning and exploring words. For a closed sort, use the bold guide words.

Words for Sorting

player	**actor**	**silken**
hunter	harden	tighten
doctor	farmer	golden
sailor	author	loser
producer	winner	awaken
operator	creator	neighbor

Take the time to discuss the puns, homophones, and figurative language presented in many of this book's word ladders. Ask students if they can generate other homophone-based puns (*a door/adore, wood/would*).

Word Ladder: Is Your Teacher Bored?

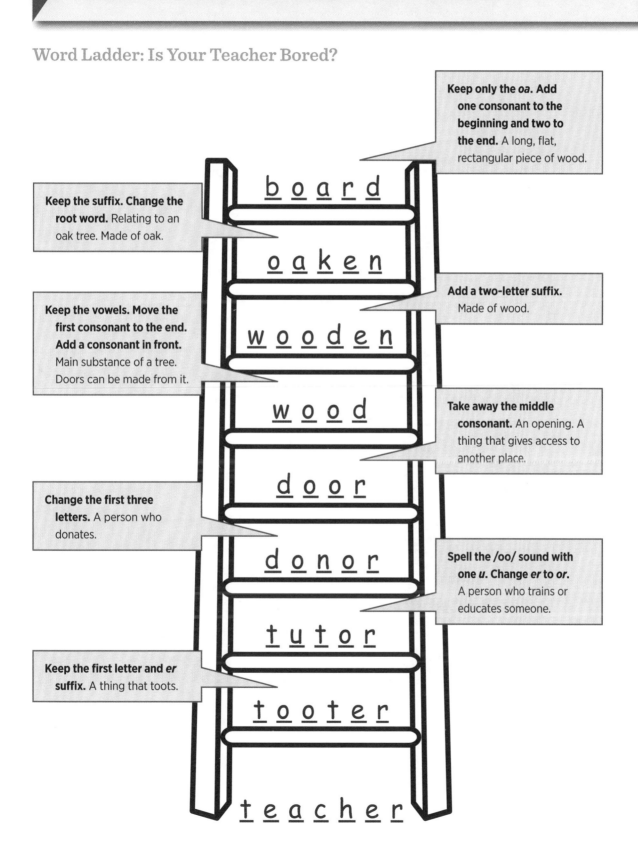

Keep only the *oa*. Add one consonant to the beginning and two to the end. A long, flat, rectangular piece of wood.

b o a r d

Keep the suffix. Change the root word. Relating to an oak tree. Made of oak.

o a k e n

Add a two-letter suffix. Made of wood.

w o o d e n

Keep the vowels. Move the first consonant to the end. Add a consonant in front. Main substance of a tree. Doors can be made from it.

w o o d

Take away the middle consonant. An opening. A thing that gives access to another place.

d o o r

Change the first three letters. A person who donates.

d o n o r

Spell the /oo/ sound with one *u*. Change *er* to *or*. A person who trains or educates someone.

t u t o r

Keep the first letter and *er* suffix. A thing that toots.

t o o t e r

t e a c h e r

Have students write with paper and pencil, whiteboard and marker, or electronic tablet.

Word Dictation

Suggested language for word dictation using the words *producer* and *dampen* as examples appears below. For additional practice, pull other words from the master spelling list.

Teacher: Get ready, everyone. The word is *producer*. Say it with me.

Students and teacher: *Producer.*

Teacher: You say it.

Students: *Producer.*

Teacher: Put your hands under your chins and say it. [Students do this.] Spell *producer*. Break it into syllables if you need to.

Students: [As students write, teacher walks among them and scans for correct and incorrect words.]

Teacher: Listen and watch: "p-r-o-d-u-c-e-r, *producer*." [Teacher writes word.] If your word is correct, give yourself a pat on the back. If it isn't correct, notice where you went wrong and correct it.

Teacher: Get ready for the next word. The word is *dampen*. Say it with me.

Students and teacher: *Dampen.*

Teacher: You say it.

Students: *Dampen.*

Teacher: Write it.

Students: [They write.]

(Continue the process and language for any other dictation words you want to give.)

Always provide correct writing and spelling after each sentence.

Sentence Dictation

Sentences for dictation and reading

The victor will be the best fighter.

He was a maker of wooden toys.

Should I tighten or loosen this bolt?

The sailor rowed an oaken boat.

He searched for a sunken chest full of golden objects.

My neighbor is an author.

A raptor is a predator.

Do you want to be pitcher or catcher?

The director directed the actors in the movie.

Every writer needs an editor.

The crane operator worked to lift the fallen load.

Suggested language for sentence dictation using *The hunter wore a woolen cap* appears below.

Teacher: Get your electronic tablets ready for writing, everyone. The sentence is *The hunter wore a woolen cap.* Say it with me.

Students and teacher: *The hunter wore a woolen cap.*

Teacher: You say it.

Students: *The hunter wore a woolen cap.*

Teacher: Write it.

Students: [As students write, teacher walks among them and scans for correct and incorrect words.]

Teacher: Listen and watch: *The hunter wore a woolen cap.* [Teacher writes sentence.] If your words are spelled correctly, you started with a capital letter, and you have a correct ending mark, give yourself a pat on the back. If your sentence isn't correct, notice where you went wrong and then fix it.

Post-Test

- At the end of your cycle of instruction, test your students by using the appropriate differentiated word list.

- Once you've effectively taught your students how to spell, not what to spell, you have the opportunity to add or substitute a word that isn't on the take-home list. For example, if *actor* was on the list, a student should also be able to spell *doctor* or *victor*.

- A post-test provides formative information. After giving the post-test, gather information about your students' needs and plan your next instructional steps.

LESSON SET 15

Focus

- Multisyllabic words with the suffix *ness*, *ment*, and *an*

Points of Instruction

- *Ness*, *ment*, and *an* are suffixes that are added to nouns.
- *Ness* means "the state or condition of" or "the quality of."
- *Ment* means "the action or state of."
- Words ending in *an* can be a noun (such as *German*, a person who lives in or is from Germany) or an adjective (such as *urban*, a word that describes an area).
- Many words formed with the *an* suffix have an *i* before the *an*. For words ending in *c* (for example, *music*, *electric*), the addition of the *i* changes the *c* sound from hard to soft (*musician*, *electrician*).

> Review or reteach any spelling concept that has not yet been mastered. Below is a list of what you may want to review or reteach.

Additional Points to Review or Reteach

- Suffixes add meaning to words.
- Words are made up of parts that have meaning. For example, the word *librarian* is made from *library*, which is a place of books and study, and the suffix *an*, which creates a new noun (a person who works in a library).
- Words with suffixes are often many syllables long.
- The strategies "See the Word in Your Head," "Spell by Analogy (Use a Word You Know)," and "Think About Meaning" can be used to spell these words.

Pre-Test

Use the pre-test in the following list to gather information about your students' needs, determine which differentiated list is appropriate for each student, and plan your next instructional steps.

> You may wish to add words that are appropriate for your students. Don't hesitate to pull in words from science and social studies.

Master Word List: *ness*, *ment*, and *an* suffix			Pre-Test List
***ness* suffix**	***ment* suffix**	***an* suffix**	
sadness	payment	magician	baldness
redness	torment	musician	illness
blackness	comment	civilian	meanness
darkness	pavement	veteran	coziness
fairness	statement	guardian	payment
baldness	movement	electrician	enjoyment
dullness	placement	comedian	amusement
illness	enjoyment	custodian	magician
shyness	repayment	librarian	civilian
dryness	replacement	urban	urban
softness	agreement	suburban	American
hardness	amusement	American	
meanness	amazement	Mexican	
niceness	alignment	Canadian	
coziness	apartment	German	
laziness			
holiness			

Consider giving your students a choice: Do they want their test to be on List A, B, or C?

Three Differentiated Word Lists		
List A	**List B**	**List C**
sadness	fairness	American
darkness	baldness	baldness
fairness	dullness	dullness
payment	pavement	enjoyment
movement	placement	alignment
illness	replacement	replacement
softness	coziness	amusement
pavement	laziness	laziness
statement	payment	amazement
musician	repayment	holiness
custodian	musician	veteran
American	custodian	guardian
shyness	American	electrician
dryness	urban	comedian
placement	suburban	Canadian

The Look Touch Say activity supports and develops the use of spelling strategies such as "Use a Word You Know" and "See the Word in Your Head."

Look Touch Say

Suggested language for practicing "See the Word in Your Head"	
sadness fairness payment torment comment civilian	**Teacher:** Look for *torment*. Touch it. [Pause.] Say it. **Students:** *Torment*. **Teacher:** See it. [They close their eyes.] Spell it by writing it down. **Students:** [They open their eyes and write it down.] **Teacher:** Look for *civilian*. Touch it. [Pause.] Say it. **Students:** *Civilian*. **Teacher:** See it. [They close their eyes.] Spell it by writing it down. **Students:** [They open their eyes and write it down.]

Suggested language for practicing "Spell by Analogy (Use a Word You Know)"	
sadness fairness payment torment comment civilian	**Teacher:** Look for two words that end with the suffix *ness*. Touch them. [Pause.] Say them. **Students:** *Sadness/fairness*. **Teacher:** If you can spell *sadness*, you can spell *madness*. Spell *madness*. **Students:** [They spell *madness*.] **Teacher:** What do *sadness* and *madness* end with, everyone? **Students:** A suffix.

Look Touch Say Extension	
Sometimes students need to practice recognizing and reading words. Here is Look Touch Say language for practicing the skill of looking for and reading words.	
sadness fairness torment comment musician civilian	**Teacher:** Look for *civilian*. Touch it. [Pause.] Say it. **Students:** *Civilian*. **Teacher:** Look for *comment*. Touch it. [Pause.] Say it. **Students:** *Comment*. **Teacher:** Look for *fairness*. Touch it. [Pause.] Say it. **Students:** *Fairness*.

Word sorts provide a great opportunity for students to notice the spelling similarities and differences between words. Encourage students to find multiple ways that words relate to one another.

Words for Sorting

sadness	**payment**	**musician**
fairness	hardness	torment
statement	magician	librarian
agreement	apartment	coziness
American	Mexican	German
laziness	softness	electrician

Do other activities, such as using phonics tiles to spell words, to teach students how one word can be transformed into another through changes in spelling.

Word Ladder: It's Magic

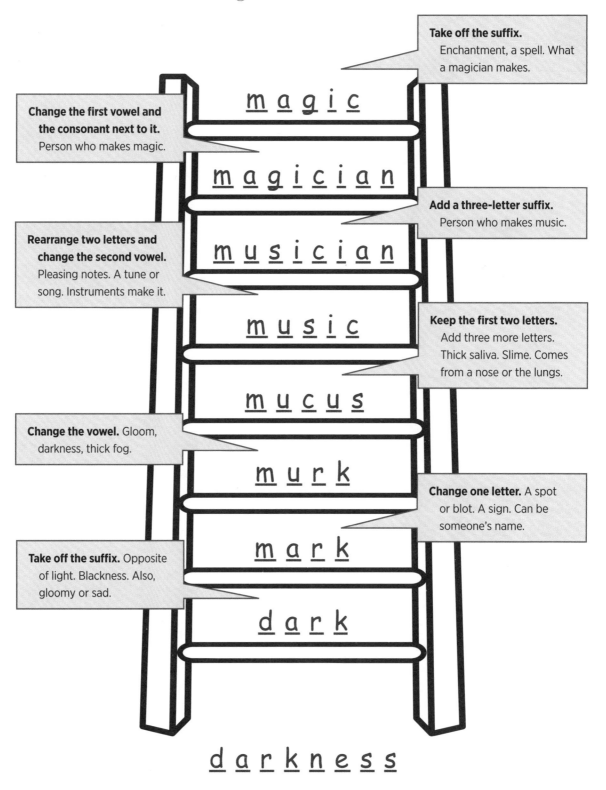

Take off the suffix. Enchantment, a spell. What a magician makes.

magic

Change the first vowel and the consonant next to it. Person who makes magic.

magician

Add a three-letter suffix. Person who makes music.

Rearrange two letters and change the second vowel. Pleasing notes. A tune or song. Instruments make it.

musician

music

Keep the first two letters. Add three more letters. Thick saliva. Slime. Comes from a nose or the lungs.

mucus

Change the vowel. Gloom, darkness, thick fog.

murk

Change one letter. A spot or blot. A sign. Can be someone's name.

mark

Take off the suffix. Opposite of light. Blackness. Also, gloomy or sad.

dark

darkness

Instant error corrections can keep mistakes from becoming permanent. Thus, providing the correct spelling after each word is an effective teaching practice.

Word Dictation

Suggested language for word dictation using the words *amazement* and *custodian* as examples appears below. For additional practice, pull other words from the master spelling list.

Teacher: Get ready, everyone. The word is *amazement*. Say it with me.

Students and teacher: *Amazement.*

Teacher: You say it.

Students: *Amazement.*

Teacher: Put your hands under your chins and say it. [Students do this.] Spell *amazement*. Break it into syllables if you need to.

Students: [As students write, teacher walks among them and scans for correct and incorrect words.]

Teacher: Listen and watch: "a-m-a-z-e-m-e-n-t, *amazement*." [Teacher writes word.] If your word is correct, give yourself a pat on the back. If it isn't correct, notice where you went wrong and correct it.

Teacher: Get ready for the next word. The word is *custodian*. Say it with me.

Students and teacher: *Custodian.*

Teacher: You say it.

Students: *Custodian.*

Teacher: Write it.

Students: [They write.]

(Continue the process and language for any other dictation words you want to give.)

More words for sentences can be found on this lesson set's master list. Use words from the master list to make your own sentences.

Sentence Dictation

Sentences for dictation and reading

The comedian made a funny comment.

His laziness drove the librarian crazy.

An electrician can light the darkness.

Many Americans live in suburban settings.

She was Mexican and he was Canadian.

He gave a statement about his baldness.

The veteran lived in an urban apartment.

The musician asked for her payment.

The librarian looked at the book in amazement.

The custodian signed a work agreement.

His guardian read his teacher's statement.

The blackness of the night made it hard to see the pavement.

Suggested language for sentence dictation using *The musician asked for her payment* appears below.

Teacher: Get your paper and pencils ready for writing, everyone. The sentence is *The musician asked for her payment.* Say it with me.

Students and teacher: *The musician asked for her payment.*

Teacher: You say it.

Students: *The musician asked for her payment.*

Teacher: Write it.

Students: [As students write, teacher walks among them and scans for correct and incorrect words.]

Teacher: Listen and watch: "The musician asked for her payment." [Teacher writes sentence.] If your words are spelled correctly, you started with a capital letter, and you have a correct ending mark, give yourself a pat on the back. If your sentence isn't correct, fix it.

Post-Test

- At the end of your cycle of instruction, test your students by using the appropriate differentiated word list.

- Once you've effectively taught your students how to spell, not what to spell, you have the opportunity to add or substitute a word that isn't on the take-home list. For example, if *sadness* was on the list, a student should also be able to spell *darkness* or *softness*.

- A post-test provides formative information. After giving the post-test, gather information about your students' needs and plan your next instructional steps.

LESSON SET 16

Focus

- Forming multisyllabic words with prefixes *pre*, *re*, and *de*

Points of Instruction

- The prefix *pre* means "before."
- The prefix *re* means "again" or "go back."
- The prefix *de* means "reduce, go away from."

> Reviewing and reteaching takes time, but it is necessary for students who have not yet mastered a skill. Centers, more complex words, and variations within activities enable you to differentiate (while you reteach), thus keeping students who have mastered the skills on track, too.

Additional Points to Review Reteach

- Prefixes add meaning to words.
- *Pre*, *re*, and *de* are all open syllables.
- Students combine the *pre*, *re*, and *de* prefixes with closed, open, vowel-team, and *r*-controlled syllables to form multisyllabic words.
- The strategies "See the Word in Your Head," "Spell by Analogy (Use a Word You Know)," and "Think About Meaning" can be used to spell these words.

Note

This lesson doesn't include suggested language for Look Touch Say, word dictation, or sentence dictation. If you have not previously used these three activities, please look to Lesson Sets 11–15 for language ideas. Use the words of your choice from this lesson's master spelling list to run the Look Touch Say and word-dictation activities. Sentences for dictation are given.

Pre-Test

Use the pre-test in the following list to gather information about your students' needs, determine which differentiated list is appropriate for each student, and plan your next instructional steps.

> *Pre*, *re*, and *de* prefixes combine with closed, open, vowel-team, and *r*-controlled syllables to form multisyllabic words. The word groupings in the master list reflect the syllable types, as well as the number of syllables.

Master Word List: *pre*, *re*, and *de* prefixes			Pre-Test List
pre prefix	*re* prefix	*de* prefix	
prefix	rerun	detect	premix
premix	refund	depend	refuse
prevent	recess	demand	pretend
precut	remind	defense	depend
pretend	refuse	deflate	prebuilt
preshrunk	remake	debate	decode
presoak	revise	decode	demand
preheat	replace	demote	decide
preteen	retire	decide	preshrunk
pretreat	refine	define	revise
prebuilt	rename	decline	recess
prepay	rewrite	derail	
	remark	defeat	
	return	decrease	
	record	delay	
	replay	deploy	
	renew	deform	
	repair	deport	
	remain	depart	
	reread	develop	
	repeat	deposit	
	recycle		

Feel free to add or subtract words based on your students' capabilities.

Three Differentiated Word Lists		
List A	List B	List C
prefix	prevent	preshrunk
premix	pretend	rewrite
refund	decide	prebuilt
depend	define	repair
pretend	decline	devoid
prevent	preheat	decrease
remake	refuse	repeat
debate	replace	recycle
refuse	rewrite	record
refine	record	deposit
retire	recess	development
deflate	pretreat	deployment
delay	prebuilt	decline
	detect	demote
	defense	revise

Words in bold can be "guide words" for a closed word sort.

Words for Sorting

preshrunk	**rename**	**decode**
return	recess	defeat
record	decrease	delay
prebuild	preteen	pretend
recycle	develop	remind
deploy	prevent	replace
repair	remain	development

Once students learn the routine, they can work on word ladders with a partner at their desk or in a word study center.

Word Ladder: Take a Test and Then Relax

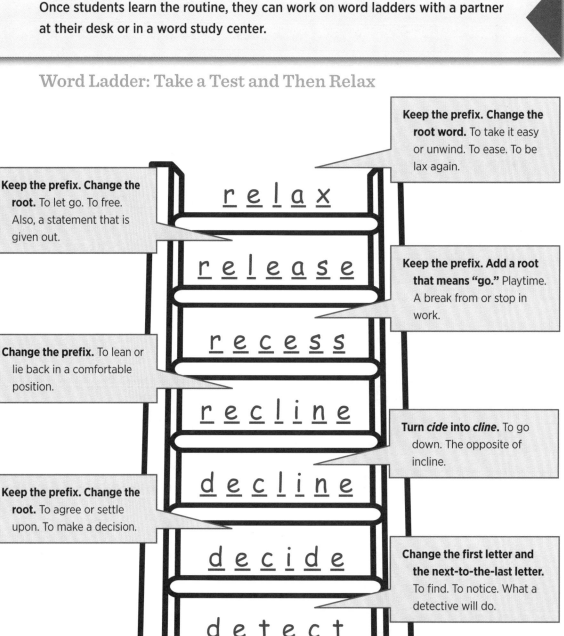

Keep the prefix. Change the root word. To take it easy or unwind. To ease. To be lax again.

r e l a x

Keep the prefix. Change the root. To let go. To free. Also, a statement that is given out.

r e l e a s e

Keep the prefix. Add a root that means "go." Playtime. A break from or stop in work.

r e c e s s

Change the prefix. To lean or lie back in a comfortable position.

r e c l i n e

Turn *cide* into *cline*. To go down. The opposite of incline.

d e c l i n e

Keep the prefix. Change the root. To agree or settle upon. To make a decision.

d e c i d e

Change the first letter and the next-to-the-last letter. To find. To notice. What a detective will do.

d e t e c t

Remove one letter to make a new prefix. To test again.

r e t e s t

Add a prefix. The test you take before the main test.

p r e t e s t

t e s t

For teacher language to use during sentence dictation, see any lesson set 12–16.

Sentence Dictation

Sentences for dictation and reading

Did you decide to take the pre-test?

Preheat the oven and thaw the precut vegetables.

Their team will return to defeat you.

I decline to decrease the payment.

Remind me to recycle the paper and glass.

The game was delayed because the football was deflated.

The preteen's jeans were preshrunk.

Did you record that remark he made?

The defense played a good game.

I will remain here and reread my book.

I decided to repair the car.

I demand that you return my book!

Can you prevent him from departing?

Did you detect a gas leak?

Don't pretend that your remark wasn't mean.

The debate is about whether we should demote him.

Post-Test

- At the end of your cycle of instruction, test your students by using the appropriate differentiated word list.

- Once you've effectively taught your students how to spell, not what to spell, you have the opportunity to add or substitute a word that isn't on the take-home list. For example, if *pre-test* was on the list, a student should also be able to spell *pretend* or *prevent*.

- A post-test provides formative information. After giving the post-test, gather information about your students' needs and plan your next instructional steps. If students did not master the spelling features presented during this instructional cycle, consider reteaching the material in the upcoming cycle.

LESSON SET 17

Focus

- Forming multisyllabic words with prefixes *mis*, *non*, and *sub*

Points of Instruction

- The prefix *mis* means "wrongly."
- The prefix *non* means "not."
- The prefix *sub* means "under."

If you are not teaching syllable types, don't worry about review terms such as *closed*, *open*, and *vowel-team syllables*.

Additional Points to Review or Reteach

- Prefixes add meaning to words.
- *Mis*, *non*, and *sub* are all closed syllables.
- Students combine the *mis*, *non*, and *sub* prefixes with closed, open, vowel-team, and *r*-controlled syllables to form multisyllabic words.
- The strategies "See the Word in Your Head," "Spell by Analogy (Use a Word You Know)," and "Think About Meaning" can be used to spell these words.

Note

This lesson doesn't include suggested language for Look Touch Say, word dictation, or sentence dictation. If you have not previously used these three activities, please look to Lesson Sets 11–15 for language ideas. Use the words of your choice from this lesson's master spelling list to run the Look Touch Say and word-dictation activities. Sentences for dictation are given.

Pre-Test

Use the pre-test in the following list to gather information about your students' needs, determine which differentiated list is appropriate for each student, and plan your next instructional steps.

Word columns are further divided by syllable types or number. For example, in the *mis* column, words are grouped by closed syllables, then closed + open syllables, then closed + vowel-team syllables, and so on.

Master Word List: prefixes			Pre-Test List
mis prefix	*non* prefix	*sub* prefix	
misfit	nonfat	subtract	misled
misled	nonstop	subtext	subtext
mistrust	nonstick	subplot	nonstick
mismatch	nonslip	subject	subject
misstep	nonsense	submit	subway
misspell	nonprofit	subway	nonsense
misuse	nondairy	subdue	misbehave
misfire	nonsmoker	subsoil	misspoke
mistake	nonverbal	subvert	submerge
misguide	noninvasive	submerge	nonviolent
misstate	nonmetallic	subheading	
misquote	nonvenomous	subzero	
misspoke	nonviolent	subtitle	
mislead		subtotal	
misread		subhuman	
misspeak		subwoofer	
mistook		submarine	
miscount		substitute	
misbehave			

You may wish to add or subtract words based on your students' capabilities.

Three Differentiated Word Lists

List A	List B	List C
misfit	misfire	misstate
misled	mistake	misquote
misspell	misspeak	misspoke
misstep	misspoke	misbehave
nonfat	mislead	nondairy
nonstop	nonsense	nonverbal
nonstick	nonprofit	noninvasive
subtract	nondairy	nonviolent
subject	nonsmoker	nonvenomous
submit	submerge	subvert
mistake	subway	subdue
nonsense	subheading	subhuman
subway	subtitle	submarine
subzero	subwoofer	substitute

Word cards from this sorting page can also be used in the flip folder center.

Words for Sorting

mistake	nonstop	subtract
subject	submit	subway
nonfat	nonsense	nonprofit
misfit	mismatch	misspell
misguide	nonsmoker	submerge
subtotal	nonmetallic	misbehave
nonslip	subdue	misspoke

Word ladders such as this one lead students to think about and manipulate the meaning-making units of words (morphemes).

Word Ladder: Watch Your Step

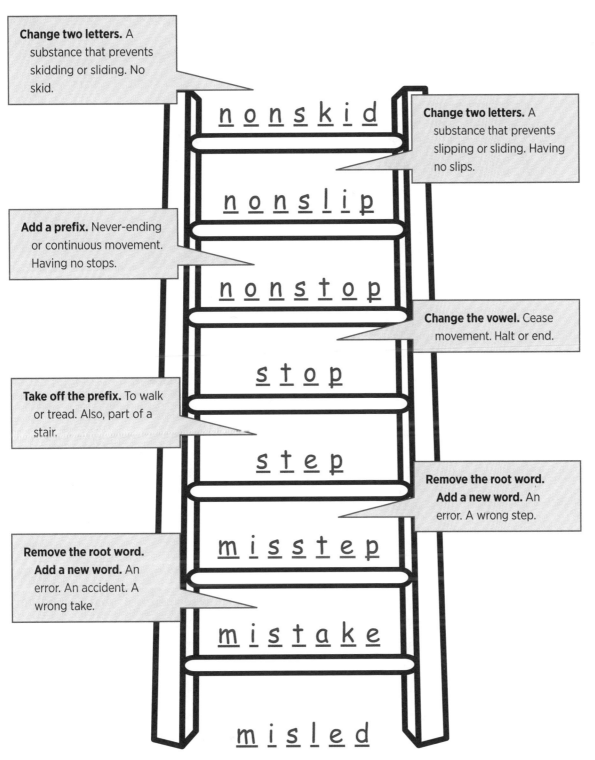

Change two letters. A substance that prevents skidding or sliding. No skid.

n o n s k i d

Change two letters. A substance that prevents slipping or sliding. Having no slips.

n o n s l i p

Add a prefix. Never-ending or continuous movement. Having no stops.

n o n s t o p

Change the vowel. Cease movement. Halt or end.

s t o p

Take off the prefix. To walk or tread. Also, part of a stair.

s t e p

Remove the root word. Add a new word. An error. A wrong step.

m i s s t e p

Remove the root word. Add a new word. An error. An accident. A wrong take.

m i s t a k e

m i s l e d

For word dictation, pull words from the master spelling list in this lesson set. Teacher language that can be used during word dictation is given in Lesson Sets 11–15.

For teacher language to use during sentence dictation, see any lesson set 12–16.

Sentence Dictation

Sentences for dictation and reading

I made a mistake and misspoke the truth.

His plan to help me misfired.

The subject of this book is a bunch of nonsense.

I mistook the subway sign for a parking sign.

The drink was nonfat and nondairy.

The two socks were mismatched.

Do you mistrust people who mislead you?

The noninvasive mushroom grew in the subsoil.

I don't think it's a mistake to be a nonsmoker.

The submarine began to submerge.

Please do not subvert the efforts of the substitute teacher.

If you misbehave, you will go to your room.

Fortunately, the snake was nonvenomous.

What are the subheading and subtitle of the story?

The subtotal is wrong because I miscounted.

Post-Test

- At the end of your cycle of instruction, test your students by using the appropriate differentiated word list.

- Once you've effectively taught your students how to spell, not what to spell, you have the opportunity to add or substitute a word that isn't on the take-home list. For example, if *mistake* was on the list, a student should also be able to spell *misfire* or *misspoke*.

- A post-test provides formative information. After giving the post-test, gather information about your students' needs and plan your next instructional steps. If students did not master the spelling features presented during this instructional cycle, consider reteaching the material in the upcoming cycle.

LESSON SET 18

Focus

- Forming multisyllabic words with prefixes *over*, *under*, and *anti*

Points of Instruction

- *Over*, *under*, and *anti* are two-syllable prefixes.
- The prefixes *over* and *under* mean what they say.
- The prefix *anti* means "against."

> You may find other concepts and features you want to review or reteach, such as the spelling of /z/: *ease* (*please*), *eeze* (*breeze, antifreeze*), *eas* (*peas, overseas*).

Additional Points to Review or Reteach

- Prefixes add meaning to words.
- Students combine the prefixes with closed, open, vowel-team, and *r*-controlled syllables to form multisyllabic words.
- The strategies "See the Word in Your Head," "Spell by Analogy (Use a Word You Know)," and "Think About Meaning" can be used to spell these words.

Note

This lesson doesn't include suggested language for Look Touch Say, word dictation, or sentence dictation. If you have not previously used these three activities, please look to Lesson Sets 11–15 for language ideas. Pick appropriate words from this lesson's master spelling list to run the Look Touch Say and word-dictation activities. Sentences for dictation are given.

Pre-Test

Use the pre-test in the following list to gather information about your students' needs, determine which differentiated list is appropriate for each student, and plan your next instructional steps.

> This list contains many syllable types such as closed, open, vowel team, vowel-consonant-e, and *r*-controlled. The word groupings in the master list reflect the syllable types as well as the number of syllables.

Master Word List: prefixes			Pre-Test List
over prefix	*under* prefix	*anti* prefix	
overpass	undercut	antiskid	overcast
overcast	underpin	antitheft	overcame
overstep	underdog	antitrust	overflow
overthink	understand	antidote	undercut
overbite	underhand	antifreeze	underwent
overtime	underwent	antiwar	antiskid
overdose	underage	antibody	antifreeze
overcame	underdone	antivirus	overseas
overcome	undertake	antibiotic	understood
overdone	undermine		antidote
overhead	understood		undermine
overheat	underwear		overhaul
overeat	underfoot		
overseas	undergo		
overhaul	undercover		
overload	underwater		
overflow	undertaker		
overproduce	underrepresent		
overprescribe			
overpopulate			
overregulate			

These differentiated words lists are not set in stone. Add or subtract words to create lists that best fit the needs of your students.

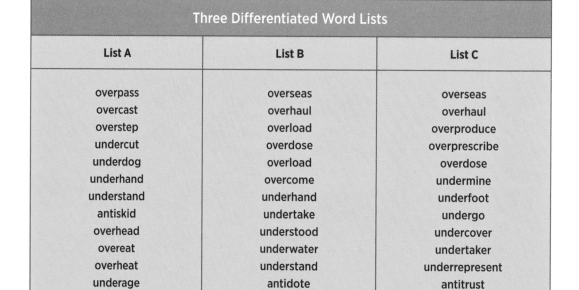

Three Differentiated Word Lists		
List A	**List B**	**List C**
overpass	overseas	overseas
overcast	overhaul	overhaul
overstep	overload	overproduce
undercut	overdose	overprescribe
underdog	overload	overdose
underhand	overcome	undermine
understand	underhand	underfoot
antiskid	undertake	undergo
overhead	understood	undercover
overeat	underwater	undertaker
overheat	understand	underrepresent
underage	antidote	antitrust
antiwar	antifreeze	antivirus
antidote	antivirus	antibiotic

Open sorts allow students to construct their own ways of understanding the relationships between words. Probe their understanding by asking "Why did you sort those words into a group?"

Words for Sorting

overcast	undercut	antiskid
overbite	overstep	antitheft
overtime	underdog	antifreeze
overload	antibiotic	overeat
antibody	undertake	undermine
understood	overhead	overhaul
overpass	underwear	undercover

Once students learn the routine, they can work on word ladders with a partner at their desk or in a word study center.

This word ladder emphasizes the manipulation of prefixes to create word meaning.

Word Ladder: Over and Under

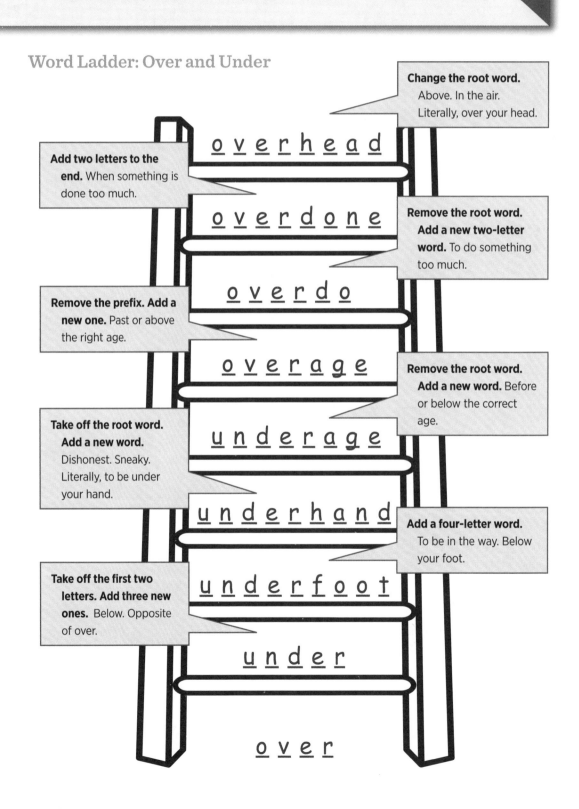

Change the root word. Above. In the air. Literally, over your head.

o v e r h e a d

Add two letters to the end. When something is done too much.

o v e r d o n e

Remove the root word. Add a new two-letter word. To do something too much.

o v e r d o

Remove the prefix. Add a new one. Past or above the right age.

o v e r a g e

Remove the root word. Add a new word. Before or below the correct age.

u n d e r a g e

Take off the root word. Add a new word. Dishonest. Sneaky. Literally, to be under your hand.

u n d e r h a n d

Add a four-letter word. To be in the way. Below your foot.

u n d e r f o o t

Take off the first two letters. Add three new ones. Below. Opposite of over.

u n d e r

o v e r

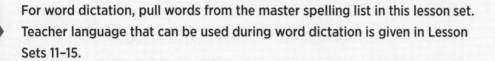

For teacher language to use during sentence dictation, see any lesson set 12–16.

For word dictation, pull words from the master spelling list in this lesson set. Teacher language that can be used during word dictation is given in Lesson Sets 11–15.

Sentence Dictation

> ### Sentences for dictation and reading
>
> Is your house near the overpass?
> I understand I should add antifreeze before winter.
> He underwent surgery and needs an antibiotic.
> Jim worked lots of overtime this year.
> Watch that you don't overheat or overcook the food.
> The weather is cool and overcast.
> The undercover cop undertook a dangerous job.
> I can't get in because I am underage.
> Prepare to undergo an overseas journey.
> Kim's old car needed an overhaul.
> The kitten was always underfoot.
> If you travel overseas, pack a lot of underwear.
> Perhaps an antivirus medicine will make you feel better.
> The truck had an antitheft device in the cab.
> Hundreds of deer overpopulated the woods.

Post-Test

- At the end of your cycle of instruction, test your students by using the appropriate differentiated word list.

- Once you've effectively taught your students how to spell, not what to spell, you have the opportunity to add or substitute a word that isn't on the take-home list. For example, if *overstep* was on the list, a student should also be able to spell *overpass* or *overthinking*.

- A post-test provides formative information. After giving the post-test, gather information about your students' needs and plan your next instructional steps. If students did not master the spelling features presented during this instructional cycle, consider reteaching the material in the upcoming cycle.

LESSON SET 19

Focus

- The Greek roots *micro, tele*, and *scope*

Points of Instruction

- Greek roots can be combined to form multisyllabic words, such as *telescope*. In *telescope*, each root has its own meaning. Both meanings combine to form a new word with a unique meaning.

- The root *micro* means "small," the root *tele* means "far," and the root *scope* means "look at or view."

> Roots are not the same as root words. Root words, such as *most* in *mostly* or *scope* in *telescope*, stand by themselves. Roots, such as *micro* and *tele*, do not stand as words by themselves.

Additional Points to Review or Reteach

- Students combine Greek roots with other Greek roots, with other types of syllables, and/or with other root words to make multisyllabic words.

- Each part of a word that holds meaning is called a morpheme. Multisyllabic words are made up of multiple morphemes. Each morpheme means something.

Note

This lesson doesn't include suggested language for Look Touch Say, word dictation, or sentence dictation. If you have not previously used these three activities, please look to Lesson Sets 11–15 for language ideas. Pick appropriate words from this lesson's master spelling list to run the Look Touch Say and word-dictation activities. Sentences for dictation are given.

Pre-Test

Use the pre-test in the following list to gather information about your students' needs, determine which differentiated list is appropriate for each student, and plan your next instructional steps.

> The English language incorporates Anglo-Saxon, Spanish, and French. It also integrates Greek and Latin. Every word in this lesson contains one or more Greek roots.

Master Word List			Pre-Test List
micro prefix	*tele* prefix	*scope* suffix	
microchip	telegram	scope	microbe
microcosm	telegraph	telescope	microchip
microsecond	telepath	microscope	microsecond
microbe	telepathic	gyroscope	telegram
microwave	teleplay	horoscope	televise
microphone	telescope	periscope	telescope
microscope	televise	stethoscope	periscope
micromanage	television	microscopic	microscope
microscopic	telephoto		
	teleprompter		
	telecommute		
	telescopic		

> Don't worry if some word lists have more words than others. Give your students spelling lists based on what they need to learn, not on what others get.

Two Differentiated Word Lists	
List A	List B
microchip	microscope
telegram	microcosm
scope	micromanage
microbe	television
microwave	telepathic
microphone	teleprompter
telescope	telecommute
televise	gyroscope
television	horoscope
telephoto	periscope
microscope	stethoscope
	microscopic

> Boldface words set up categories for a word sort. Ask students, "Where does *telescope* belong, under *scope* or *telegram*?" Answers may vary. To understand student thinking, ask students, "Why did you sort the word this way?" and "What is your thinking behind your choice?"

Words for Sorting

microbe	telegram	scope
microchip	teleplay	gyroscope
periscope	microwave	telescope
telegraph	stethoscope	microphone
telepathic	microscope	telephoto
television	televise	micromanage

You may need to teach and/or expand on word meanings (such as for the word *strobe*).

Tele and *micro* are Latin roots. The majority of the time their position is in front of another root or root word. Thus, they also function as prefixes.

Word Ladder: Scope This Out

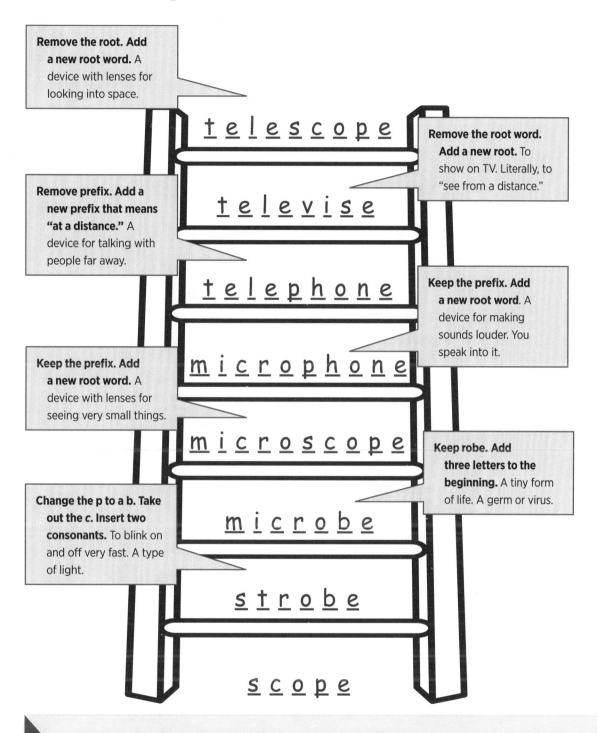

Remove the root. Add a new root word. A device with lenses for looking into space.

t e l e s c o p e

Remove the root word. Add a new root. To show on TV. Literally, to "see from a distance."

Remove prefix. Add a new prefix that means "at a distance." A device for talking with people far away.

t e l e v i s e

t e l e p h o n e

Keep the prefix. Add a new root word. A device for making sounds louder. You speak into it.

Keep the prefix. Add a new root word. A device with lenses for seeing very small things.

m i c r o p h o n e

m i c r o s c o p e

Keep robe. Add three letters to the beginning. A tiny form of life. A germ or virus.

Change the p to a b. Take out the c. Insert two consonants. To blink on and off very fast. A type of light.

m i c r o b e

s t r o b e

s c o p e

For word dictation, pull words from the master spelling list in this lesson set. Teacher language for word dictation is given in Lesson Sets 11–15.

For teacher language to use during sentence dictation, see any lesson set 12–16.

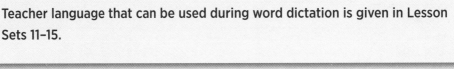

For word dictation, pull words from the master spelling list in this lesson set. Teacher language that can be used during word dictation is given in Lesson Sets 11–15.

Sentence Dictation

Sentences for dictation and reading

Microbes live everywhere.

The microchip in the microwave must be broken.

Speak into the microphone.

They will televise the game at noon.

He used a telephoto lens and a strobe light to shoot the picture.

For her television speech, she used a teleprompter.

Doctor Wilson used a stethoscope during his examination.

I can see the stars through the telescope.

The submarine raised its periscope.

Workers do not like to be micromanaged.

Like a telepath, she knew what I was going to say.

He used a microscope to view the microbes.

To do his job, Jim telecommutes from home.

A broken gyroscope meant the plane could not fly.

She wrote a teleplay for the television show.

The microbe was microscopic.

Before texts, people used telegrams and telephones.

Post-Test

- At the end of your cycle of instruction, test your students by using the appropriate differentiated word list.

- Once you've effectively taught your students how to spell, not what to spell, you have the opportunity to add or substitute a word that isn't on the take-home list. For example, if *telephone* was on the list, a student should also be able to spell *televise* or *telescope*.

- A post-test provides formative information. After giving the post-test, gather information about your students' needs and plan your next instructional steps. If students did not master the spelling features presented during this instructional cycle, consider reteaching the material in the upcoming cycle.

LESSON SET 20

Focus

- The Greek roots *bio*, *graph*, *photo*, and *auto*

Points of Instruction

- Greek roots are sometimes combined to form multisyllabic words, such as *autobiography*. In *autobiography*, each root has its own meaning. All three meanings combine to form a new word that has a unique meaning.

- The root *bio* means "life." The root *graph* means "draw or write." The root *photo* means "light." The root *auto* means "self" or "directed from within."

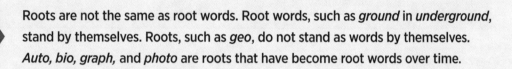

Roots are not the same as root words. Root words, such as *ground* in *underground*, stand by themselves. Roots, such as *geo*, do not stand as words by themselves. *Auto, bio, graph,* and *photo* are roots that have become root words over time.

Additional Points to Review or Reteach

- Students combine Greek roots with other Greek roots, with other types of syllables, and/or with other root words to make multisyllabic words.

- Each part of a word that holds meaning is called a morpheme. Multisyllabic words are made up of multiple morphemes. Each morpheme means something.

- The strategies "See the Word in Your Head," "Spell by Analogy (Use a Word You Know)," and "Think About Meaning" can be used to spell these words.

Note

This lesson doesn't include suggested language for Look Touch Say, word dictation, or sentence dictation. If you have not previously used these three activities, please look to Lesson Sets 11–15 for language ideas. Pick appropriate words from this lesson's master spelling list to run the Look Touch Say and word-dictation activities. Sentences for dictation are given.

Pre-Test

Use the pre-test in the following list to gather information about your students' needs, determine which differentiated list is appropriate for each student, and plan your next instructional steps.

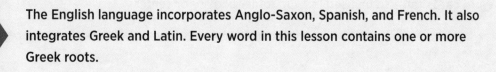

The English language incorporates Anglo-Saxon, Spanish, and French. It also integrates Greek and Latin. Every word in this lesson contains one or more Greek roots.

Master Word List				Pre-Test List
bio	*graph*	*photo*	*auto*	
biosphere	graph	photo	auto	biosphere
biofuel	graphic	photon	automate	biography
biography	graphite	photograph	autograph	graphic
biology	photograph	photocopy	autopilot	paragraph
symbiotic	autograph	telephoto	autofocus	photography
bioscience	paragraph	photocopier	automation	autograph
probiotic	telegraph	photoelectric	automatic	photocopier
biohazard	photographic	photosynthesis	automobile	autopilot
	geographic		autobiography	bioscience
	photography			autobiography
	biography			
	autobiography			

List assignments are never permanent. A student who gets a B list may later get an A list, and vice versa.

Two Differentiated Word Lists	
List A	**List B**
graph	autograph
graphic	photographic
autograph	geographic
paragraph	biography
photograph	autobiography
biosphere	biosphere
biography	biology
photo	symbiotic
photon	biohazard
photocopy	photocopier
photocopier	photoelectric
auto	photosynthesis
autograph	automate
automobile	automation
	automatic

Word cards can also be used in a flip folder activity or center.

Words for Sorting

auto	photo	graph
bio	biology	graphic
graphite	photon	biofuel
biography	telephoto	paragraph
autograph	bioscience	photoelectric
photocopy	photographic	biohazard
geographic	autobiographic	probiotic

▶ Students can team up to complete word ladders or do them as a whole group.

Word Ladder: This Is Your Life

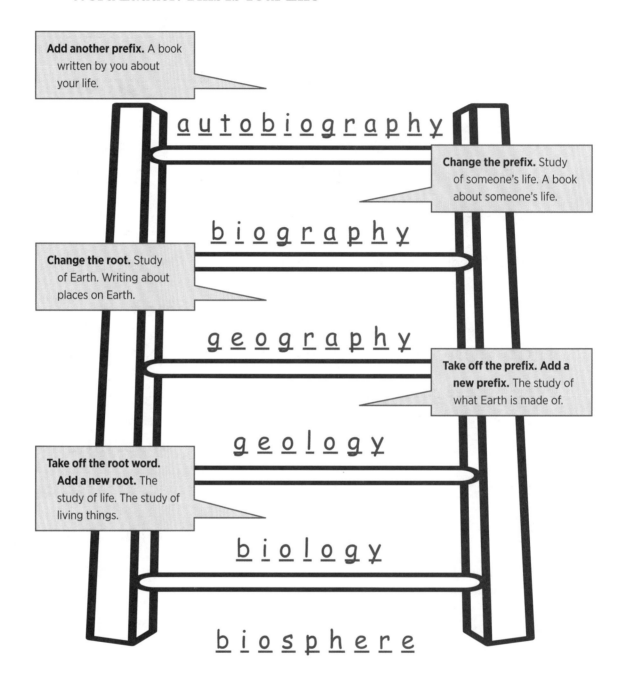

Add another prefix. A book written by you about your life.

autobiography

Change the prefix. Study of someone's life. A book about someone's life.

biography

Change the root. Study of Earth. Writing about places on Earth.

geography

Take off the prefix. Add a new prefix. The study of what Earth is made of.

geology

Take off the root word. Add a new root. The study of life. The study of living things.

biology

biosphere

For word dictation, pull words from the master spelling list in this lesson set. Teacher language for word dictation is given in Lesson Sets 11–15.

Don't forget about the reading part. Warm up by having students read decodable sentences.

For teacher language to use during sentence dictation, see any lesson set 12–16.

Sentence Dictation

Sentences for dictation and reading

Did you use a telephoto lens to take that photograph?

Use the photocopier to make a photocopy.

Biology is an important field of science.

The publisher of my book about biofuels asked for my bio.

If your gut is upset, take a probiotic.

Her autobiography is five hundred pages long.

The pilot put the plane on autopilot.

I prefer to travel by automobile.

The automobile used biofuel.

May I have your autograph?

Plants use photosynthesis to make energy.

Automation is replacing jobs.

The pencil was made of wood and graphite.

Is your writing at least four paragraphs long?

Post-Test

- At the end of your cycle of instruction, test your students by using the appropriate differentiated word list.

- Once you've effectively taught your students how to spell, not what to spell, feel free to add or substitute a word that isn't on the take-home list. For example, if *graph* was on the list, a student should also be able to spell *graphic* or *graphite*.

- A post-test provides formative information. After giving the post-test, gather information about your students' needs and plan your next instructional steps. If students did not master the spelling features presented during this instructional cycle, consider reteaching the material in the upcoming cycle.

LESSON SET 21

Focus

- The Latin roots *ject*, *rupt*, *uni*, and *act*

Points of Instruction

- Latin roots are sometimes combined to form multisyllabic words, such as *unicorn*. In *unicorn*, each root has its own meaning.

- The root *ject* means "throw." The root *rupt* means "break." The root *uni* means "one." The root *act* means "do."

> Roots are not the same as root words. Root words, such as *most* in *mostly*, stand by themselves. Roots, such as *ject* and *uni*, do not stand as words by themselves.

Additional Points to Review or Reteach

- Students combine Latin roots with other types of syllables, with prefixes and suffixes, and/or with other root words to make multisyllabic words.

- Each part of a word that holds meaning is called a morpheme. Multisyllabic words are made up of multiple morphemes. Each morpheme holds meaning.

- The strategies "See the Word in Your Head," "Spell by Analogy (Use a Word You Know)," and "Think About Meaning" can be used to spell these words.

Note

This lesson doesn't include suggested language for Look Touch Say, word dictation, or sentence dictation. If you have not previously used these three activities, please look to Lesson Sets 11–15 for language ideas. Pick appropriate words from this lesson's master spelling list to run the Look Touch Say and word-dictation activities. Sentences for dictation are given.

Pre-Test

Use the pre-test in the following list to gather information about your students' needs, determine which differentiated list is appropriate for each student, and plan your next instructional steps.

> The English language incorporates Anglo-Saxon, Spanish, and French. It also integrates Greek and Latin. Every word in this lesson contains one or more Latin roots.

Master Word List:				Pre-Test List
ject	*rupt*	*uni*	*act*	
object	bankrupt	unit	act	subject
subject	corrupt	unite	action	project
inject	erupt	union	actor	injection
project	abrupt	unison	react	bankrupt
eject	disrupt	reunion	enact	disrupt
deject	rupture	universe	active	eruption
reject	disruptive	unisex	inactive	unite
injection	corruption	unicorn	counteract	universe
objection	eruption	united	reaction	unify
projection	abruptly	uniform	activate	action
ejection	interrupt	unify	overactive	inactive
rejection	interruption	unicycle	activism	activate
projectile	incorruptible	universal	retroactive	
projector		United States	deactivate	
objective		university	hyperactive	
subjective			radioactive	
adjective				
trajectory				

◀ Consider giving your students a choice: Do they want their test to be on List A, B, or C?

Three Differentiated Word Lists

List A	List B	List C
object	subject	projection
subject	project	injection
eject	projection	projectile
project	injection	trajectory
projection	disruption	disruption
disrupt	bankrupt	bankrupt
bankrupt	disruptive	interruption
erupt	corrupt	corrupt
unit	corruption	incorruptible
unite	united	unite
united	United States	unify
United States	union	university
act	reunion	reunion
action	action	hyperactive
actor	inactive	deactivate
active	activate	radioactive

Students can take home a word card sheet, cut the words apart, and ask family members how they would sort the words.

Words for Sorting

inject	erupt	unit
act	object	bankrupt
union	injection	disrupt
unison	unicorn	rupture
activate	counteract	reject
unify	abrupt	interrupt
projection	unicycle	universal

Do you know why the unicorn is dejected? It's because no one *believes* in her!

Uni is a Latin root. The majority of the time its position is in front of another root or root word. Thus, it is also a prefix.

Word Ladder: The Dejected Unicorn

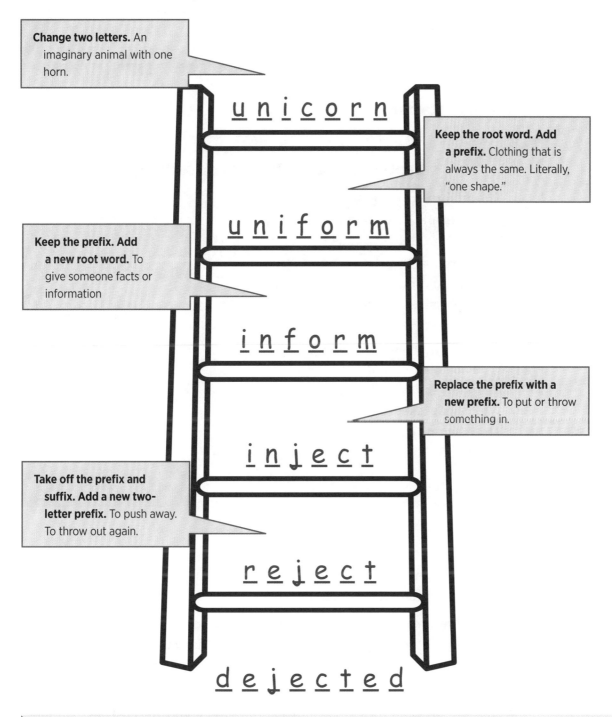

Change two letters. An imaginary animal with one horn.

Keep the root word. Add a prefix. Clothing that is always the same. Literally, "one shape."

Keep the prefix. Add a new root word. To give someone facts or information

Replace the prefix with a new prefix. To put or throw something in.

Take off the prefix and suffix. Add a new two-letter prefix. To push away. To throw out again.

u n i c o r n

u n i f o r m

i n f o r m

i n j e c t

r e j e c t

d e j e c t e d

For word dictation, pull words from the master spelling list in this lesson set. Teacher language for word dictation is given in Lesson Sets 12–16.

Gather formative assessment data on sentence dictation. Consider giving longer or shorter sentences if the word is too easy or difficult for students.

For teacher language to use during sentence dictation, see any lesson set 12–16.

Sentence Dictation

Sentences for dictation and reading

The uniformed nurse gave me an injection.
Your corrupt company will go bankrupt.
The volcanic eruption ended abruptly.
The projectile traveled on a high trajectory.
His interruptions disrupted the class.
The universe is an active place.
Radioactive water spilled from the ruptured pipeline.
She was hyperactive and disruptive.
What is the subject of your project?
He rode a unicycle and she rode a unicorn.
When her project was rejected, she felt dejected.
The injection caused a reaction.
What is the best university in the United States?
Her overacting was like an eruption of feeling.

Post-Test

- At the end of your cycle of instruction, test your students by using the appropriate differentiated word list.

- Once you've effectively taught your students how to spell, not what to spell, you have the opportunity to add or substitute a word that isn't on the take-home list. For example, if *object* was on the list, a student should also be able to spell *inject* or *subject*.

- A post-test provides formative information. After giving the post-test, gather information about your students' needs and plan your next instructional steps. If students did not master the spelling features presented during this instructional cycle, consider reteaching the material in the upcoming cycle.

Creating Your Own Lesson Sets

The time has come to consider making your own lesson sets. Because this book is not a spelling program, you'll need additional lesson sets to teach your spelling content. But you don't need to create lesson sets that look exactly like the ones here, nor do you need to begin with entire sets. You can begin by infusing ideas in this book into the lessons you already teach. For example, start by making sure your cycle of spelling instruction isn't teaching too many spelling features. I suggest spelling lessons focus on two to four features. If most of your students are in the earlier stages of spelling development, consider focusing on two spelling features. If they are in the later stages of development, consider three or four features.

Next, add words built on the spelling feature(s) you are focusing on to create a master list. Then do any of the following: (1) Give a pre-test at the beginning of your teaching cycle and use that information to develop ways of differentiating; (2) replace some of your worksheets with whole-group spelling activities like Look Touch Say, word dictation, and word sorts; or (3) use different words (pulled from your enhanced master list of spelling words) in each activity, center, and test. Once you have one new routine or have incorporated new material into your lesson, try incorporating more the next week or the next month.

If you do want to create entire lesson sets that follow the spirit of this book, here is a recap of the ingredients you will need to cook up your own series of lessons:

- A spelling scope and sequence

- Two to four spelling features to teach per cycle of instruction

- A deep and rich master list of words built on the spelling features you've chosen

- A spelling pre-test that allows you to gauge student knowledge before you begin your instruction

- Differentiated word lists for groups of kids to take home and study

- Materials for spelling activities: spelling words on cards, word lists for Look Touch Say, at least two or three sentences for sentence dictation

- Knowledge of how to run the various activities (Look Touch Say, word sorts, word dictation, sentence dictation, and so forth)

- Optional materials and tools such as flip folders; letter or word "chunk" tiles; whiteboards for writing; electronic tablets for writing/typing; word ladders; word lists and clipboards for buddies to give practice tests; and so on

- A spelling post-test that allows you to gauge student knowledge after you have given instruction

To help you create lesson sets, a lesson planning template is in Appendix I. On the template are all the components of a Super Spellers Lesson Set, including the important points you want to teach and remember, places to create a master list, a pre-test list, sentences for dictation, the words you want to have your students sort, and so forth.

Unlike the lessons provided in this book, which all have the same components, your lesson sets may look different from week to week. Find a groove or keep changing things up (which can be refreshing for both you and your students). You decide how you want to introduce the spelling feature, which lesson components you will use, and how much time you will give to any particular activity or opportunity for direct and explicit instruction.

Scope and Sequence

The first bullet point above—a scope and sequence—is the only one this book hasn't discussed in depth. A scope and sequence is an organizational tool that allows you to track your instruction, follow the progress of your students along a continuum of development, and modify your instruction based on that progress. If you are teaching spelling and phonics without a scope and sequence, I recommend you get one or, if you have the experience and the knowledge to do so, create one. You can get one by

- borrowing one from a recently published reading series;

- reconfiguring one from an older reading series;

- creating one using your school district's standards as a guide;

- creating one specific to your grade level from one of the general scope and sequences in Appendix H;

- creating one using the developmental continuum and the spelling features from a detailed spelling inventory; or

- using the scope and sequence of syllable types, as outlined in an encoding-decoding program such as Wilson Reading or as briefly outlined in Appendix H of this book.

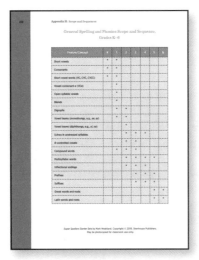

Scope and Sequence

If you have a basal program, you have a spelling scope and sequence. You also have a phonics scope and sequence. Because encoding and decoding are two sides of the same coin (the alphabetic principle), phonics and spelling should march down the road arm in arm, in lockstep. There should be no difference between your spelling scope and sequence and your phonics scope and sequence. At some point you should determine for yourself if your spelling and phonics scope and sequences are aligned. If they don't match, I suggest you seriously consider reconfiguring them so that they do. Instruction is more powerful when spelling and phonics concepts follow the same sequence and children are explicitly taught that spelling is for reading.

Finally, here are a few additional suggestions for how to think about teaching your scope and sequence, no matter where it comes from. Each of these points is discussed in depth in the third chapter of my book *Super Spellers: Seven Steps to Transforming Your Spelling Instruction*.

- Commit to teaching short vowel sounds to mastery.

- Spend more time teaching vowel sounds and patterns and less time teaching consonant sounds and patterns.

- Consider teaching the seven syllable types. Also consider planning horizontally and vertically with other teachers to create a way to teach the seven syllable types across the grade levels.

When thinking about your spelling scope and sequence, don't forget that spelling achievement follows a developmental path, not a grade-level path. This means that students exhibit different levels of spelling mastery within any given grade and any given classroom. If many of your fourth-grade students are struggling to read and write, teach and reteach spelling features typically taught in second or third grade. If you have a classroom of high-flying third graders who are exceptional spellers, concentrate on prefixes, suffixes, and Greek and Latin roots and root words. The key is to give your students what they need, when they need it. That isn't dictated by some universally imposed, one-size-fits-all scope and sequence. Rather, it is based on formative assessment data, as well as your teacher sense of what your students know and don't know.

Hear and spell sounds.

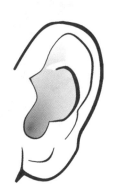

/m/ /a/ /p/

map

Use a word you know.

moon

spoon

cartoon

See the word in your head.

explore

Think about meaning.

Make a memory aid.

"A fri**end** to the **end**."

"The princi**pal** is your **pal**."

Circle, come back, correct.

Appendix B: Spelling Grids

Spelling Strategy Classroom Survey Sheet

Directions

- To determine use of strategies, ask the students, "How did you spell that word?" "What strategy did you use?" "Why did you spell it that way?"
- If you see and hear evidence that a particular strategy is being used, check the appropriate box. You may want to mark it IP (in progress) or E (established). A survey of your entire class may take you three to four weeks.
- *H & S* stands for the Hear and Spell the Sounds strategy.

	Student	Date	Strategies				
			H & S*	Analogy	Sight	Mnemonic	Meaning
1							
2							
3							
4							
5							
6							
7							
8							
9							
10							
11							
12							
13							
14							
15							
16							
17							
18							
19							
20							
21							
22							
23							
24							
25							
26							
27							
28							
29							
30							

Circle, Come Back, Correct Strategy Classroom Survey Sheet

Directions

- Using student samples of writing, ask yourself these questions: Did the student attempt the strategy? Are there three to five words circled? Have the circled words been corrected?
- Using your own criteria, determine if the student is using the strategy effectively, somewhat (in progress), or not at all.

★ = effective use   ✔ = in progress   O = no use

	Student	Date the Use of Strategy Was Assessed			
1					
2					
3					
4					
5					
6					
7					
8					
9					
10					
11					
12					
13					
14					
15					
16					
17					
18					
19					
20					
21					
22					
23					
24					
25					
26					
27					
28					
29					
30					

Folder Master

Flip Folder Directions

Step 1

- Pick up a spelling word card. **Say** the word on the card.

- **See** the word in your mind. Notice the patterns of the word.

Step 2

- Lift the left flap and put the word card on the folder. Put the flap down to **hide** the word.

- **See** the word in your head.

Step 3

- Pick up the right flap, put a blank slip of paper down, and **write** the spelling word.

Step 4

- Lift the left flap and **check** your word against the word card. If your spelling isn't correct, **correct** your mistake. If your spelling is correct, put a check mark or draw a star on your slip.

- Put the spelling card back in its pile. Put the spelling word you wrote to the side.

- Close both flaps, pick a new spelling word card, and start again!

- When you are finished, staple all the words you wrote together, put your name on top, and put them into the work basket.

Write
Check
Correct

Say
See
- - -
Hide
See

Appendix E: Tumble Block Template

Word Hunt

Name _____   Date _____

Book _____

Find and list words with the following patterns:

_____

Primary Word Scavenger Hunt

Name _____   Date _____

Book _____

Number of words to find in each category: 1   2   3   4   5

Search for . . .	Words (with page number)
Words with short vowel sounds *a e i o u*	
Words with digraph *ck th ch sh*	
Words with blends *sl fl gr cr*	
Words with vowel-consonant-e *a-e i-e o-e u-e*	
Words with "-ng" patterns *ing ong ang ung*	

Intermediate Word Scavenger Hunt

Completed by _____   Date _____

Book used   _____

Target number of words: 1   2   3   4   5

Search for . . .	Words (with page number)
Words with open syllables	
Words with vowel teams *oa ou oi oy oo* *ee ea eigh ew* *ay ai aw* *ue ui*	
Words with prefixes *pre di ex dis* *un re con*	
Words with suffixes *er ment ness tion* *ate ize ly* *able ful ic less*	

Lesson Set 1

Turn a Cat into a Dog

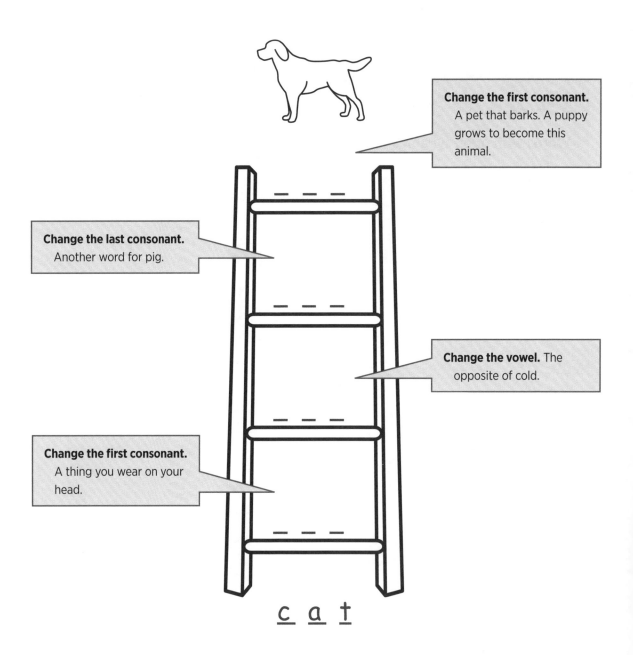

Change the first consonant. A pet that barks. A puppy grows to become this animal.

Change the last consonant. Another word for pig.

Change the vowel. The opposite of cold.

Change the first consonant. A thing you wear on your head.

c a t

Lesson Set 1

Turn Dad into a Frog

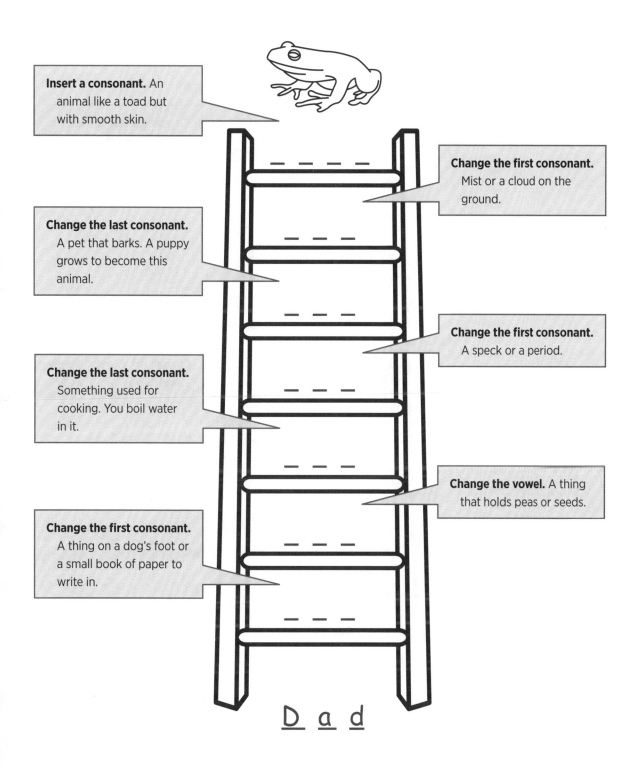

Insert a consonant. An animal like a toad but with smooth skin.

Change the first consonant. Mist or a cloud on the ground.

Change the last consonant. A pet that barks. A puppy grows to become this animal.

Change the first consonant. A speck or a period.

Change the last consonant. Something used for cooking. You boil water in it.

Change the vowel. A thing that holds peas or seeds.

Change the first consonant. A thing on a dog's foot or a small book of paper to write in.

D a d

Lesson Set 2

Turn a Pig into a Duck

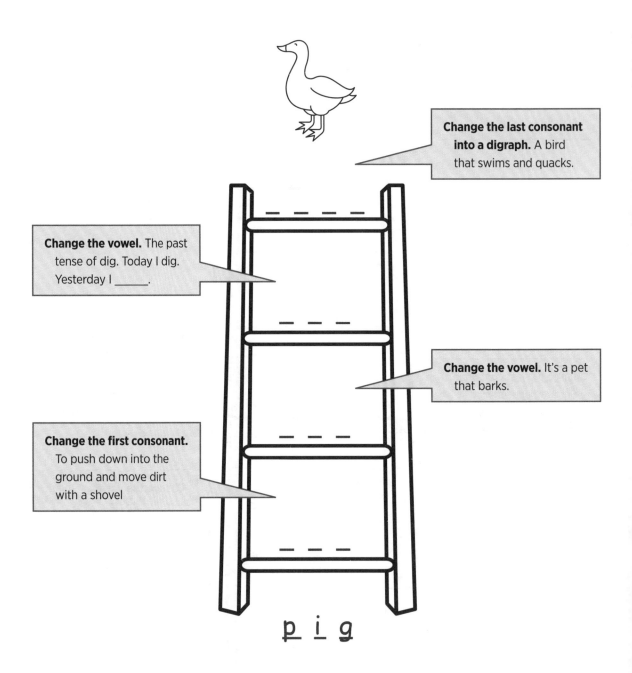

Change the last consonant into a digraph. A bird that swims and quacks.

Change the vowel. The past tense of dig. Today I dig. Yesterday I _____.

Change the vowel. It's a pet that barks.

Change the first consonant. To push down into the ground and move dirt with a shovel

p i g

Lesson Set 2

Bug on a Twig

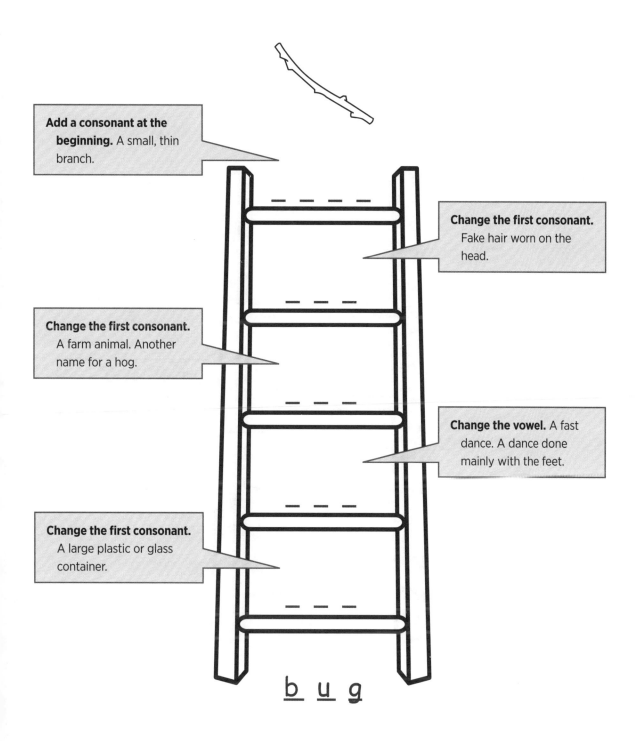

Add a consonant at the beginning. A small, thin branch.

Change the first consonant. Fake hair worn on the head.

Change the first consonant. A farm animal. Another name for a hog.

Change the vowel. A fast dance. A dance done mainly with the feet.

Change the first consonant. A large plastic or glass container.

b u g

Lesson Set 3

Make Jill the Boss

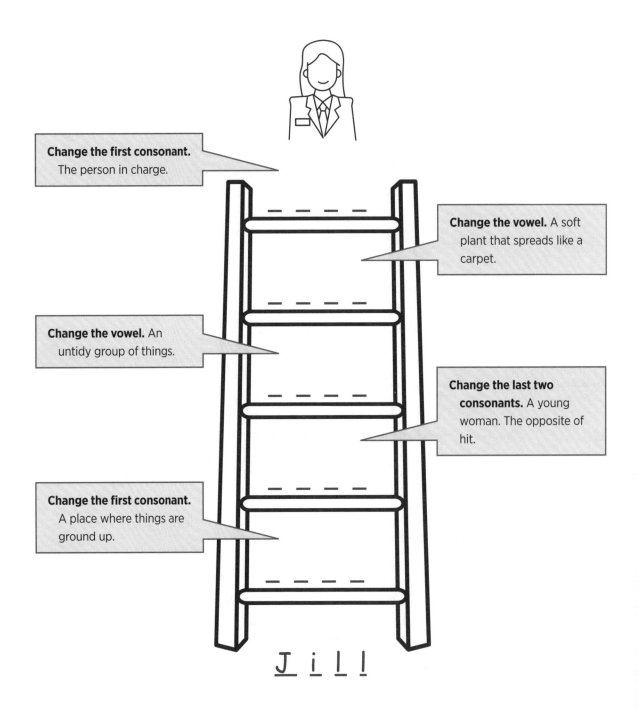

Change the first consonant. The person in charge.

Change the vowel. A soft plant that spreads like a carpet.

Change the vowel. An untidy group of things.

Change the last two consonants. A young woman. The opposite of hit.

Change the first consonant. A place where things are ground up.

J i l l

Lesson Set 3

Huff and Puff up the Hill

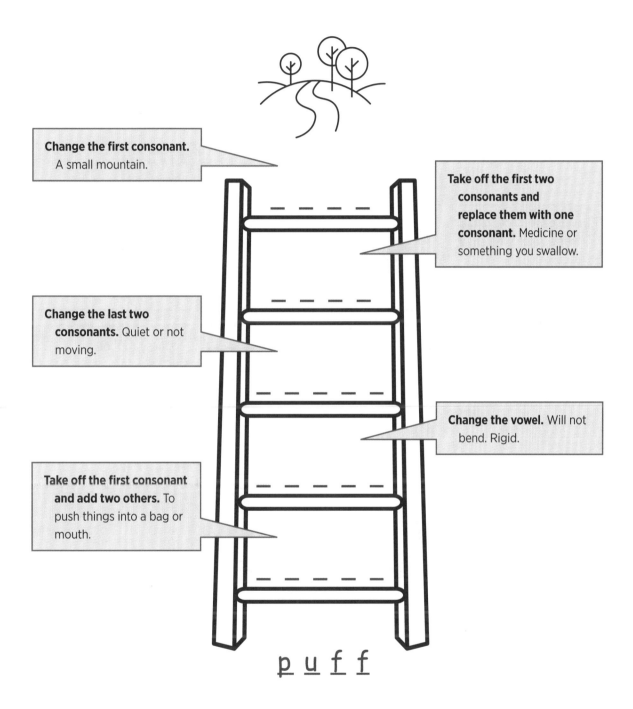

Change the first consonant. A small mountain.

Take off the first two consonants and replace them with one consonant. Medicine or something you swallow.

Change the last two consonants. Quiet or not moving.

Change the vowel. Will not bend. Rigid.

Take off the first consonant and add two others. To push things into a bag or mouth.

p u f f

Lesson Set 4

Find a Jackpot in Your Backpack

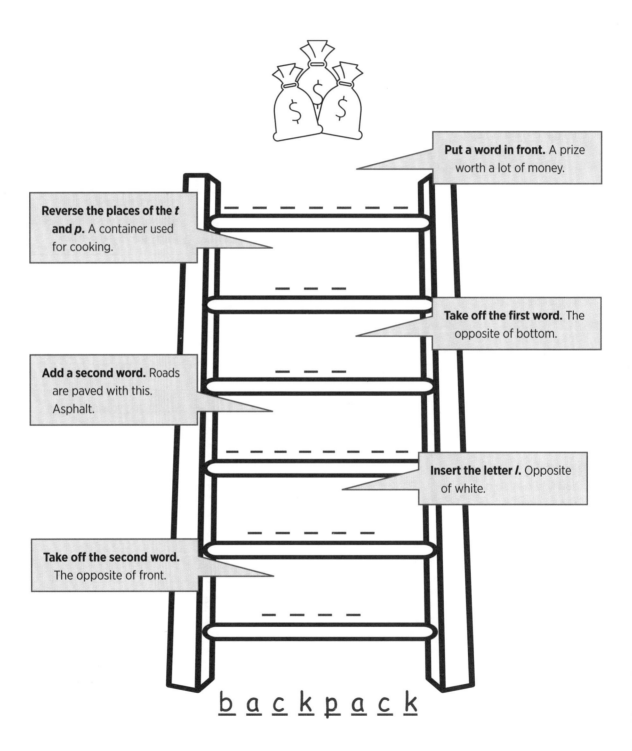

Put a word in front. A prize worth a lot of money.

Reverse the places of the *t* and *p*. A container used for cooking.

Take off the first word. The opposite of bottom.

Add a second word. Roads are paved with this. Asphalt.

Insert the letter *l*. Opposite of white.

Take off the second word. The opposite of front.

b a c k p a c k

Lesson Set 4

Catnip for the Tomcat

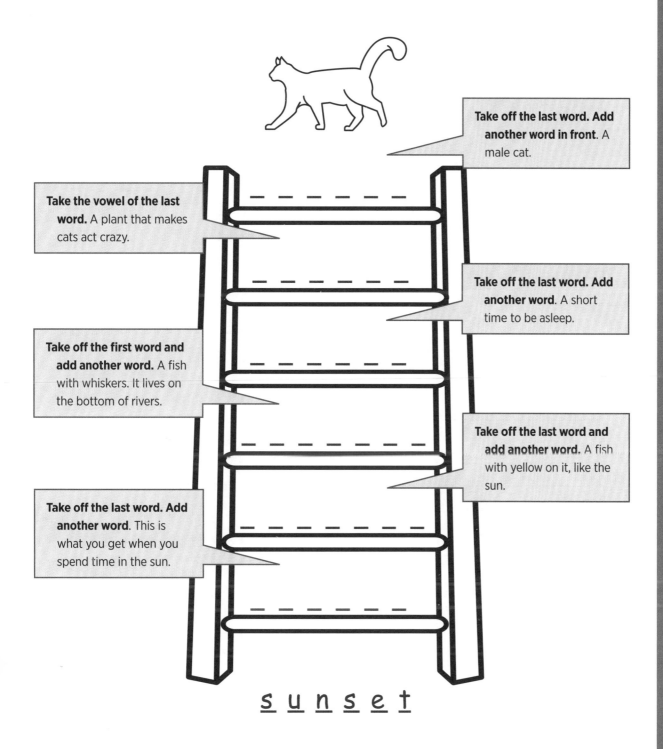

Take off the last word. Add another word in front. A male cat.

Take the vowel of the last word. A plant that makes cats act crazy.

Take off the last word. Add another word. A short time to be asleep.

Take off the first word and add another word. A fish with whiskers. It lives on the bottom of rivers.

Take off the last word and add another word. A fish with yellow on it, like the sun.

Take off the last word. Add another word. This is what you get when you spend time in the sun.

s u n s e t

Lesson Set 5

Rope a Hog

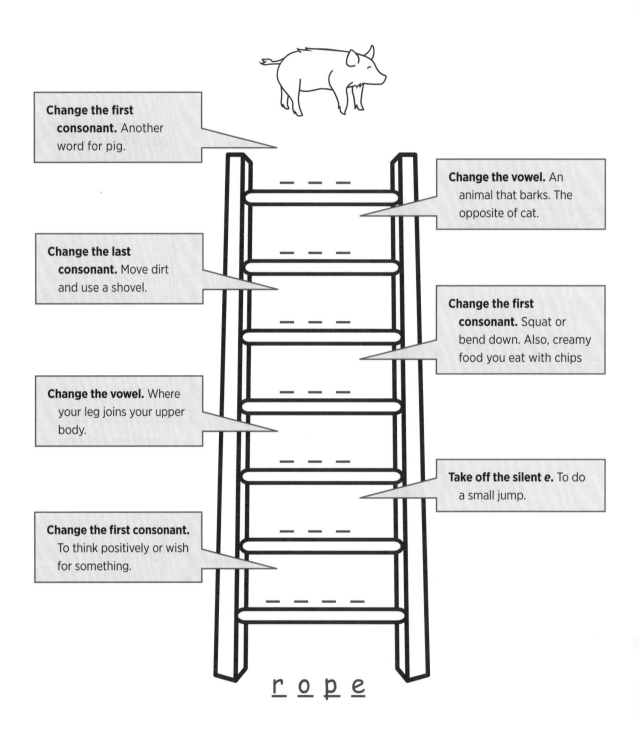

Change the first consonant. Another word for pig.

Change the vowel. An animal that barks. The opposite of cat.

Change the last consonant. Move dirt and use a shovel.

Change the first consonant. Squat or bend down. Also, creamy food you eat with chips

Change the vowel. Where your leg joins your upper body.

Take off the silent e. To do a small jump.

Change the first consonant. To think positively or wish for something.

r o p e

Lesson Set 5

Hop on a Plane

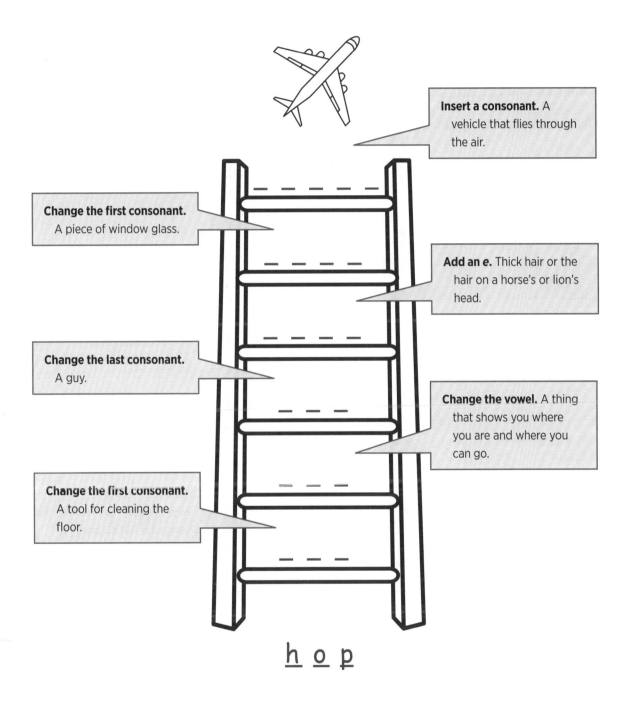

Insert a consonant. A vehicle that flies through the air.

Change the first consonant. A piece of window glass.

Add an e. Thick hair or the hair on a horse's or lion's head.

Change the last consonant. A guy.

Change the vowel. A thing that shows you where you are and where you can go.

Change the first consonant. A tool for cleaning the floor.

h o p

Lesson Set 6

Turn a Kid into a Cube

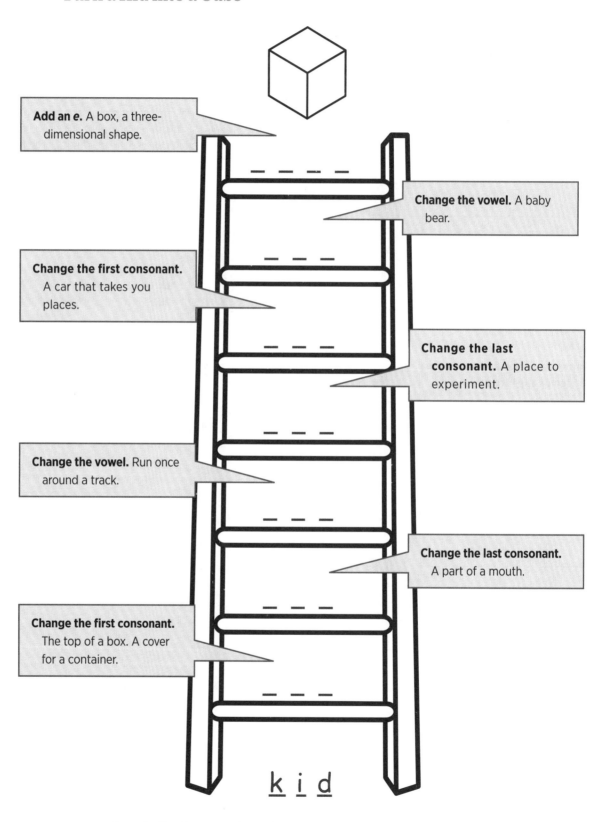

Add an e. A box, a three-dimensional shape.

Change the vowel. A baby bear.

Change the first consonant. A car that takes you places.

Change the last consonant. A place to experiment.

Change the vowel. Run once around a track.

Change the last consonant. A part of a mouth.

Change the first consonant. The top of a box. A cover for a container.

k i d

Lesson Set 6

Turn a Nut into a Pine

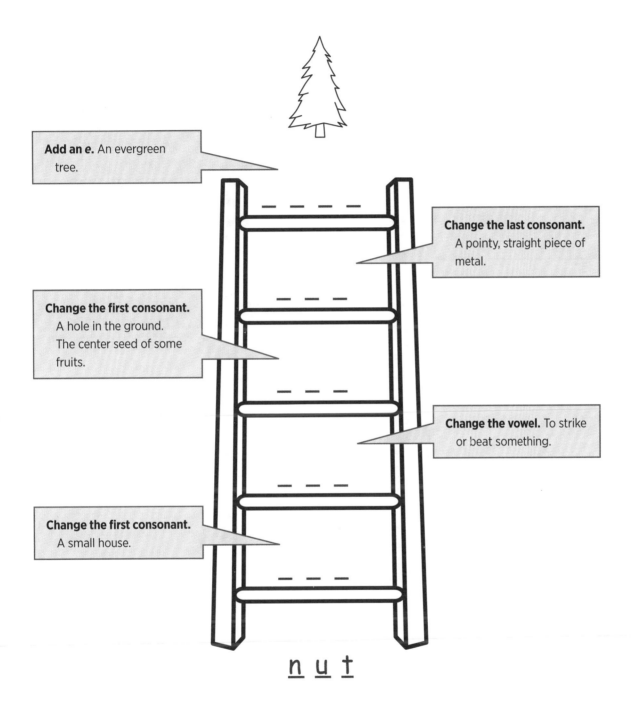

Add an e. An evergreen tree.

Change the last consonant. A pointy, straight piece of metal.

Change the first consonant. A hole in the ground. The center seed of some fruits.

Change the vowel. To strike or beat something.

Change the first consonant. A small house.

n u t

Lesson Set 7

Turn Sharks into Ferns

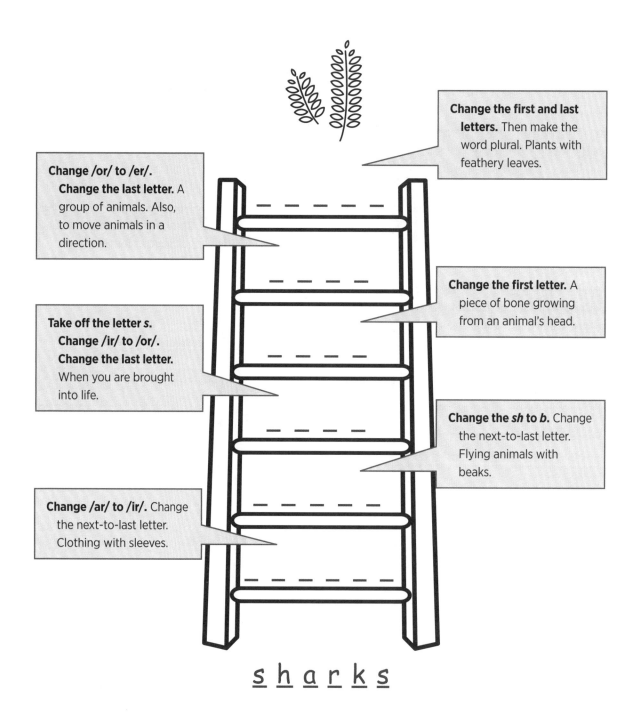

Change /or/ to /er/. Change the last letter. A group of animals. Also, to move animals in a direction.

Take off the letter *s*. Change /ir/ to /or/. Change the last letter. When you are brought into life.

Change /ar/ to /ir/. Change the next-to-last letter. Clothing with sleeves.

Change the first and last letters. Then make the word plural. Plants with feathery leaves.

Change the first letter. A piece of bone growing from an animal's head.

Change the *sh* to *b*. Change the next-to-last letter. Flying animals with beaks.

<u>s</u> <u>h</u> <u>a</u> <u>r</u> <u>k</u> <u>s</u>

Lesson Set 8

Bird Word

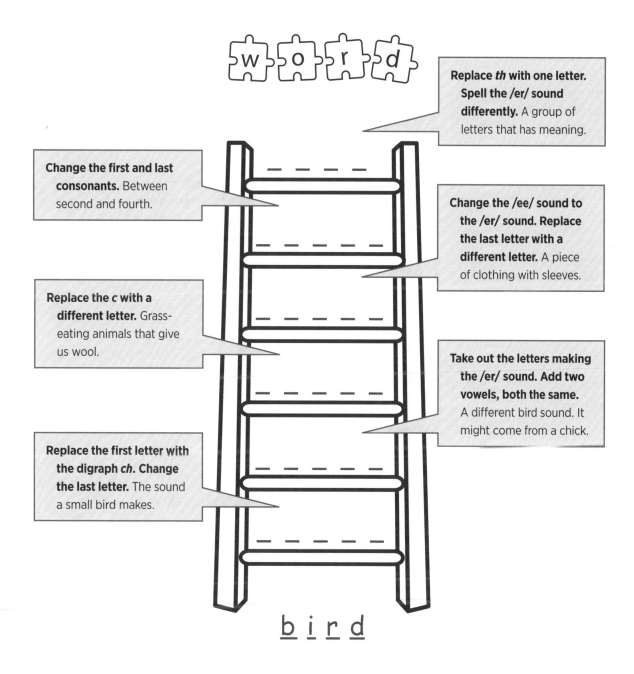

Replace *th* with one letter. **Spell the /er/ sound differently.** A group of letters that has meaning.

Change the first and last consonants. Between second and fourth.

Change the /ee/ sound to the /er/ sound. Replace the last letter with a different letter. A piece of clothing with sleeves.

Replace the *c* with a different letter. Grass-eating animals that give us wool.

Take out the letters making the /er/ sound. Add two vowels, both the same. A different bird sound. It might come from a chick.

Replace the first letter with the digraph *ch*. Change the last letter. The sound a small bird makes.

Lesson Set 9

Foiled Again

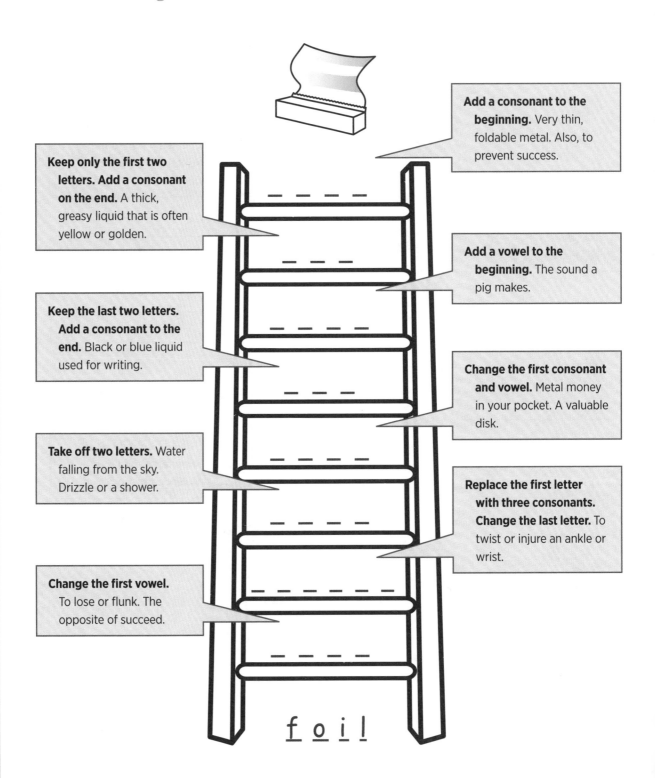

Add a consonant to the beginning. Very thin, foldable metal. Also, to prevent success.

Keep only the first two letters. Add a consonant on the end. A thick, greasy liquid that is often yellow or golden.

Add a vowel to the beginning. The sound a pig makes.

Keep the last two letters. Add a consonant to the end. Black or blue liquid used for writing.

Change the first consonant and vowel. Metal money in your pocket. A valuable disk.

Take off two letters. Water falling from the sky. Drizzle or a shower.

Replace the first letter with three consonants. Change the last letter. To twist or injure an ankle or wrist.

Change the first vowel. To lose or flunk. The opposite of succeed.

f o i l

Lesson Set 10

The Snowy Goat

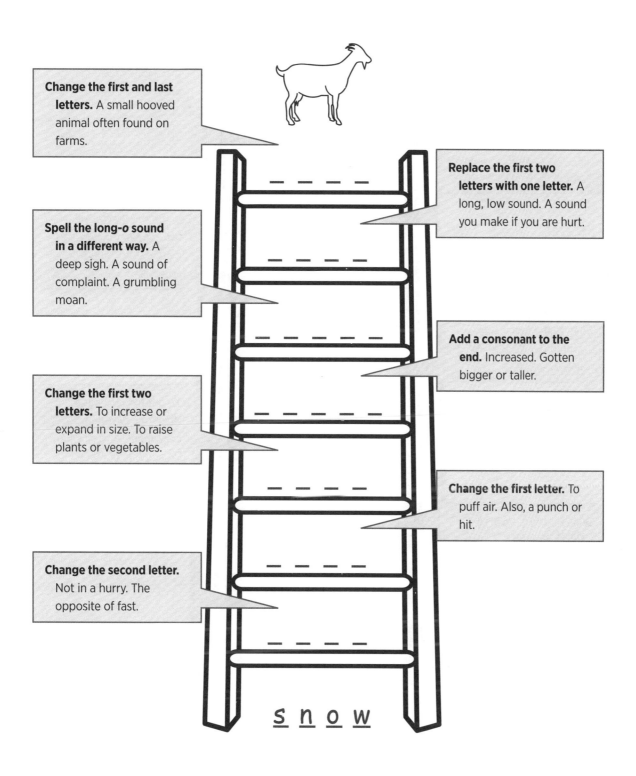

Change the first and last letters. A small hooved animal often found on farms.

Replace the first two letters with one letter. A long, low sound. A sound you make if you are hurt.

Spell the long-*o* sound in a different way. A deep sigh. A sound of complaint. A grumbling moan.

Add a consonant to the end. Increased. Gotten bigger or taller.

Change the first two letters. To increase or expand in size. To raise plants or vegetables.

Change the first letter. To puff air. Also, a punch or hit.

Change the second letter. Not in a hurry. The opposite of fast.

s n o w

Lesson Set 11

A Light in the Jungle

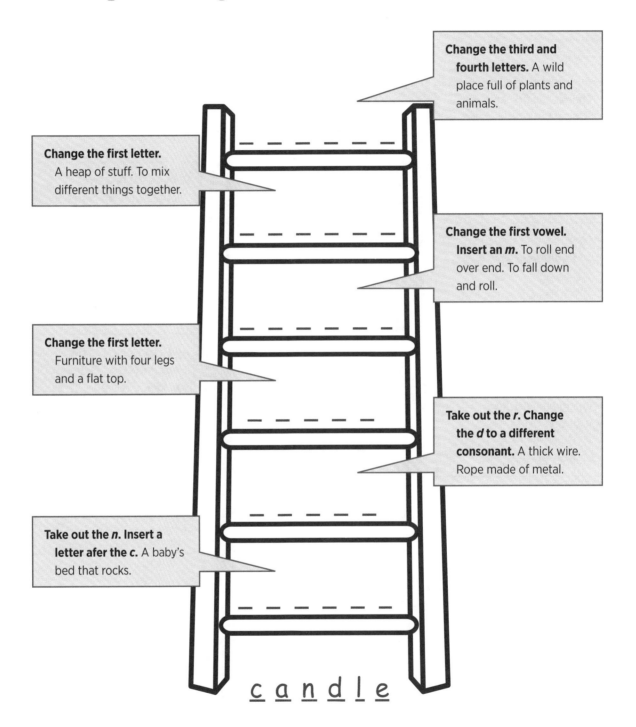

Change the third and fourth letters. A wild place full of plants and animals.

Change the first letter. A heap of stuff. To mix different things together.

Change the first vowel. Insert an *m*. To roll end over end. To fall down and roll.

Change the first letter. Furniture with four legs and a flat top.

Take out the *r*. Change the *d* to a different consonant. A thick wire. Rope made of metal.

Take out the *n*. Insert a letter afer the *c*. A baby's bed that rocks.

c a n d l e

Lesson Set 12

Battle an Eagle

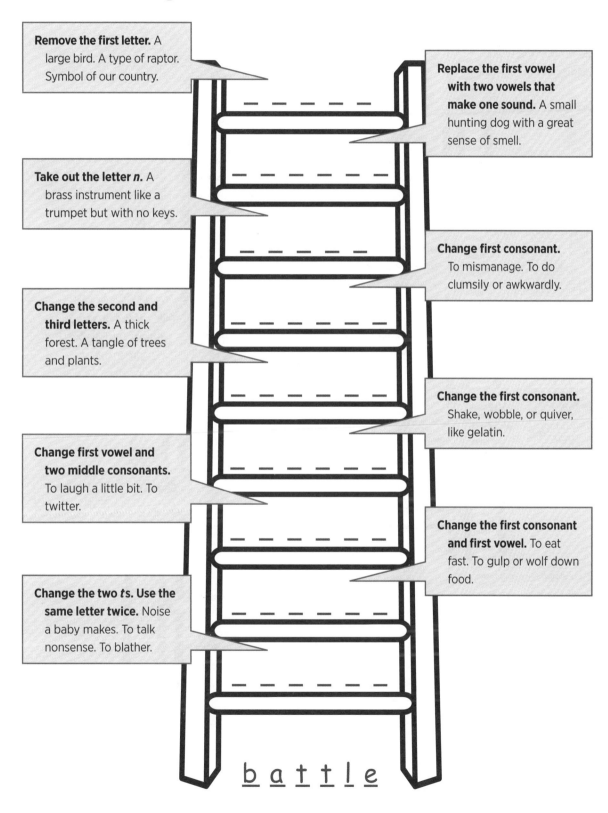

Remove the first letter. A large bird. A type of raptor. Symbol of our country.

Replace the first vowel with two vowels that make one sound. A small hunting dog with a great sense of smell.

Take out the letter *n*. A brass instrument like a trumpet but with no keys.

Change first consonant. To mismanage. To do clumsily or awkwardly.

Change the second and third letters. A thick forest. A tangle of trees and plants.

Change the first consonant. Shake, wobble, or quiver, like gelatin.

Change first vowel and two middle consonants. To laugh a little bit. To twitter.

Change the first consonant and first vowel. To eat fast. To gulp or wolf down food.

Change the two *t*s. Use the same letter twice. Noise a baby makes. To talk nonsense. To blather.

b a t t l e

Lesson Set 13

Don't Be a Couch Potato

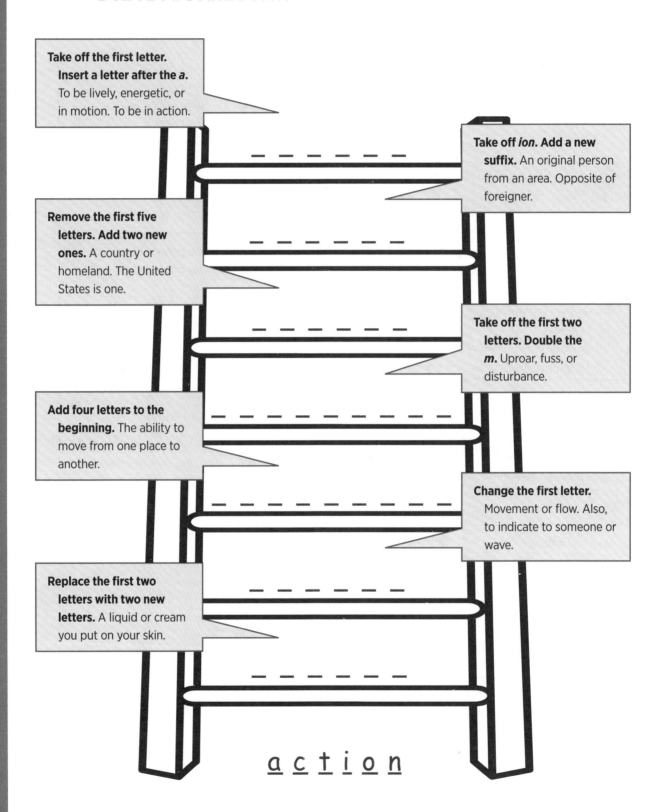

Take off the first letter. Insert a letter after the *a*. To be lively, energetic, or in motion. To be in action.

Take off *ion*. Add a new suffix. An original person from an area. Opposite of foreigner.

Remove the first five letters. Add two new ones. A country or homeland. The United States is one.

Take off the first two letters. Double the *m*. Uproar, fuss, or disturbance.

Add four letters to the beginning. The ability to move from one place to another.

Change the first letter. Movement or flow. Also, to indicate to someone or wave.

Replace the first two letters with two new letters. A liquid or cream you put on your skin.

a c t i o n

Lesson Set 14

Is Your Teacher Bored?

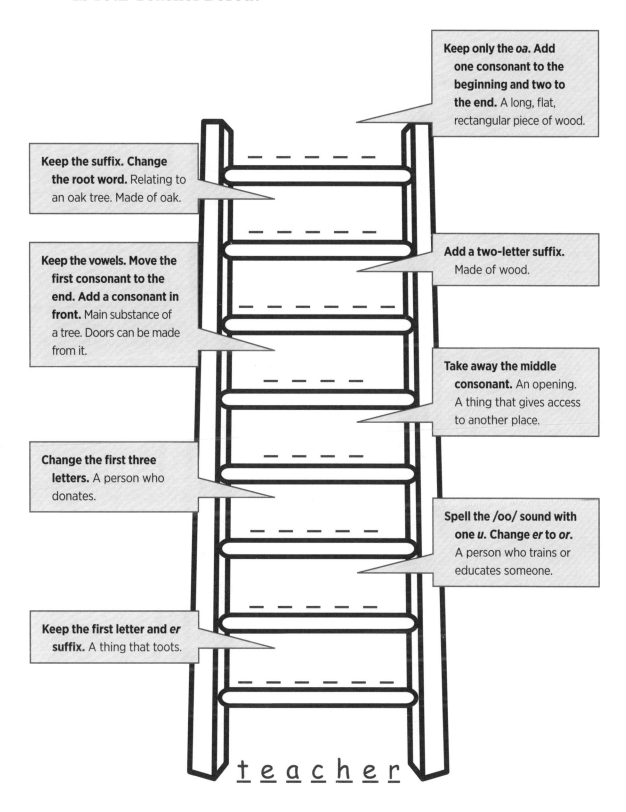

Keep only the *oa*. Add one consonant to the beginning and two to the end. A long, flat, rectangular piece of wood.

Keep the suffix. Change the root word. Relating to an oak tree. Made of oak.

Add a two-letter suffix. Made of wood.

Keep the vowels. Move the first consonant to the end. Add a consonant in front. Main substance of a tree. Doors can be made from it.

Take away the middle consonant. An opening. A thing that gives access to another place.

Change the first three letters. A person who donates.

Spell the /oo/ sound with one *u*. Change *er* to *or*. A person who trains or educates someone.

Keep the first letter and *er* suffix. A thing that toots.

t e a c h e r

Lesson Set 15

It's Magic

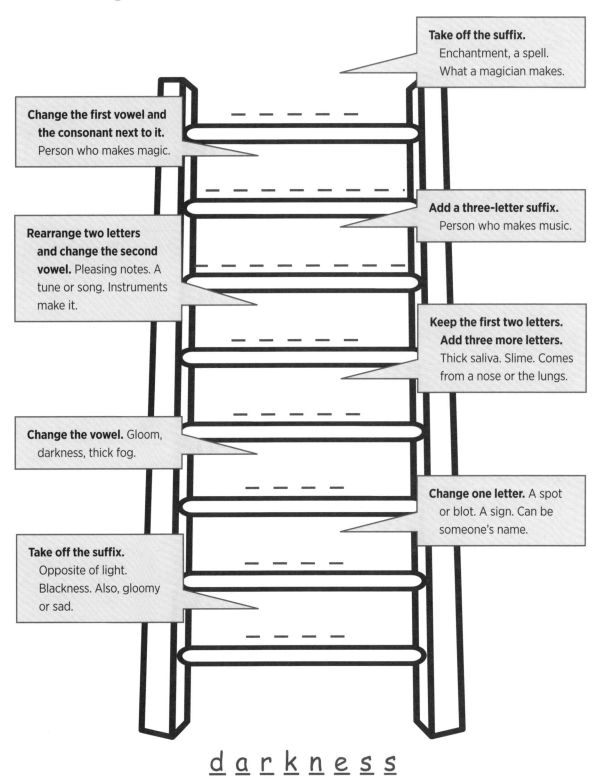

Take off the suffix.
Enchantment, a spell.
What a magician makes.

Change the first vowel and the consonant next to it. Person who makes magic.

Add a three-letter suffix.
Person who makes music.

Rearrange two letters and change the second vowel. Pleasing notes. A tune or song. Instruments make it.

Keep the first two letters. Add three more letters. Thick saliva. Slime. Comes from a nose or the lungs.

Change the vowel. Gloom, darkness, thick fog.

Change one letter. A spot or blot. A sign. Can be someone's name.

Take off the suffix.
Opposite of light.
Blackness. Also, gloomy or sad.

d a r k n e s s

Lesson Set 16

Take a Test and Then Relax

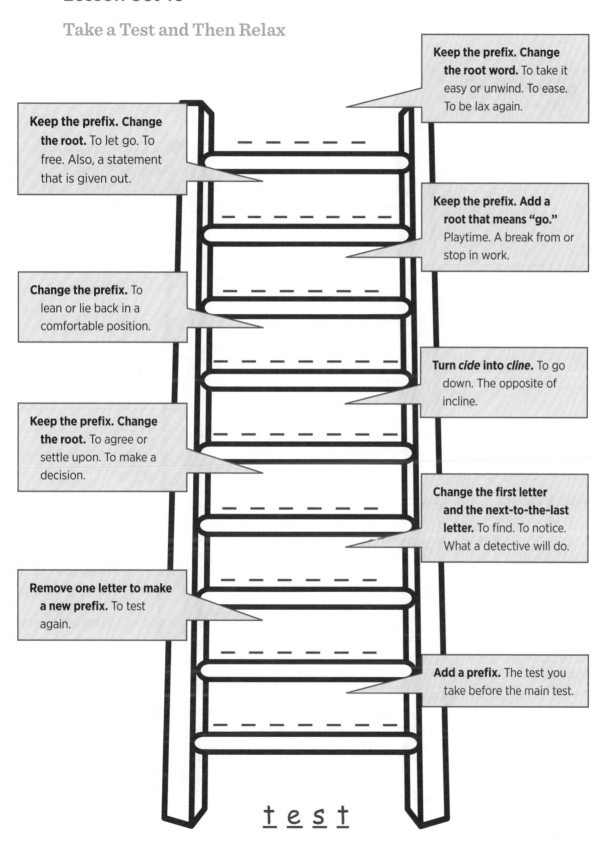

Keep the prefix. Change the root word. To take it easy or unwind. To ease. To be lax again.

Keep the prefix. Change the root. To let go. To free. Also, a statement that is given out.

Keep the prefix. Add a root that means "go." Playtime. A break from or stop in work.

Change the prefix. To lean or lie back in a comfortable position.

Turn *cide* into *cline*. To go down. The opposite of incline.

Keep the prefix. Change the root. To agree or settle upon. To make a decision.

Change the first letter and the next-to-the-last letter. To find. To notice. What a detective will do.

Remove one letter to make a new prefix. To test again.

Add a prefix. The test you take before the main test.

t e s t

Lesson Set 17

Watch Your Step

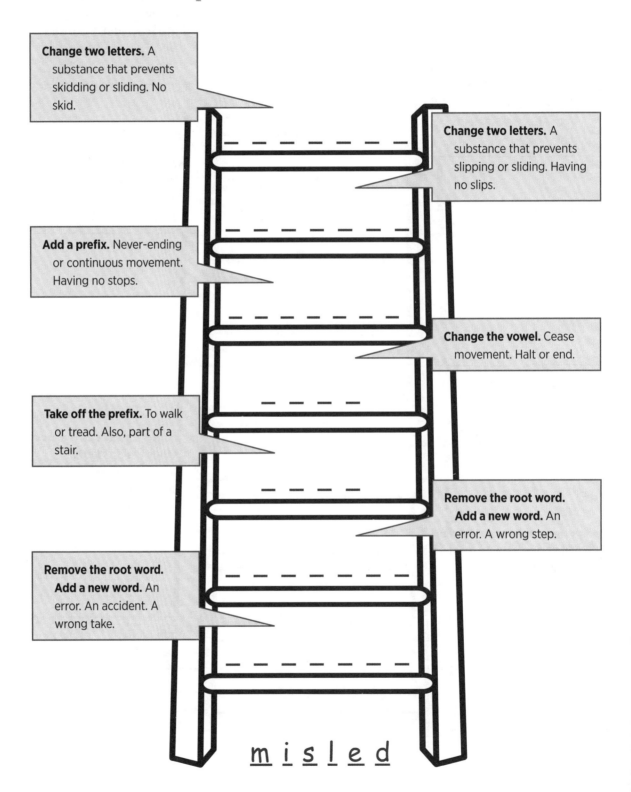

Change two letters. A substance that prevents skidding or sliding. No skid.

Change two letters. A substance that prevents slipping or sliding. Having no slips.

Add a prefix. Never-ending or continuous movement. Having no stops.

Change the vowel. Cease movement. Halt or end.

Take off the prefix. To walk or tread. Also, part of a stair.

Remove the root word. Add a new word. An error. A wrong step.

Remove the root word. Add a new word. An error. An accident. A wrong take.

m i s l e d

Lesson Set 18

Over and Under

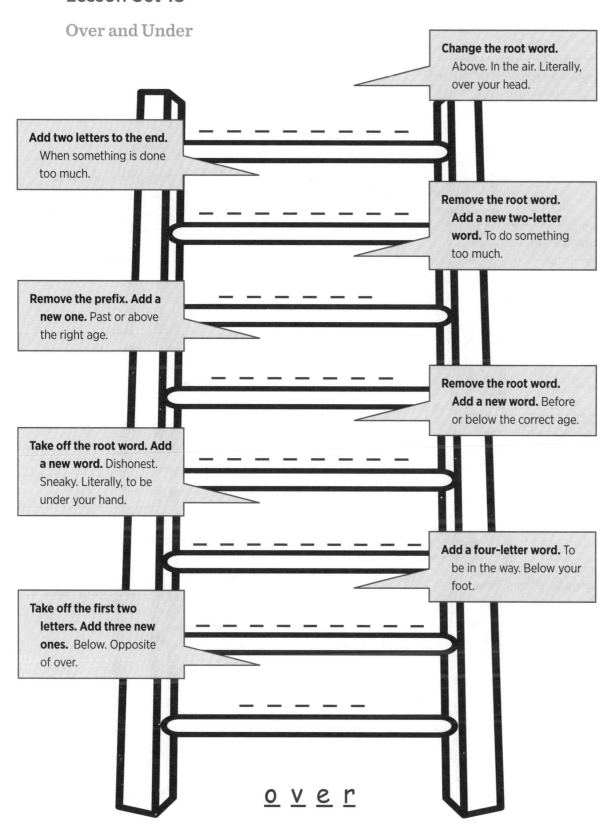

Change the root word. Above. In the air. Literally, over your head.

Add two letters to the end. When something is done too much.

Remove the root word. Add a new two-letter word. To do something too much.

Remove the prefix. Add a new one. Past or above the right age.

Remove the root word. Add a new word. Before or below the correct age.

Take off the root word. Add a new word. Dishonest. Sneaky. Literally, to be under your hand.

Add a four-letter word. To be in the way. Below your foot.

Take off the first two letters. Add three new ones. Below. Opposite of over.

o v e r

Lesson Set 19

Scope This Out

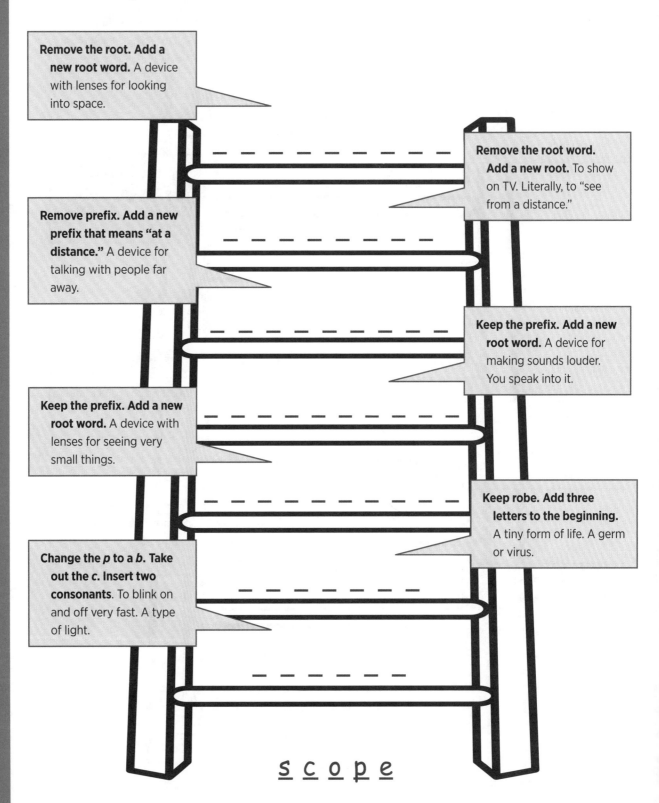

Remove the root. Add a new root word. A device with lenses for looking into space.

Remove the root word. Add a new root. To show on TV. Literally, to "see from a distance."

Remove prefix. Add a new prefix that means "at a distance." A device for talking with people far away.

Keep the prefix. Add a new root word. A device for making sounds louder. You speak into it.

Keep the prefix. Add a new root word. A device with lenses for seeing very small things.

Keep robe. Add three letters to the beginning. A tiny form of life. A germ or virus.

Change the *p* to a *b*. Take out the *c*. Insert two consonants. To blink on and off very fast. A type of light.

s c o p e

Lesson Set 20

This Is Your Life

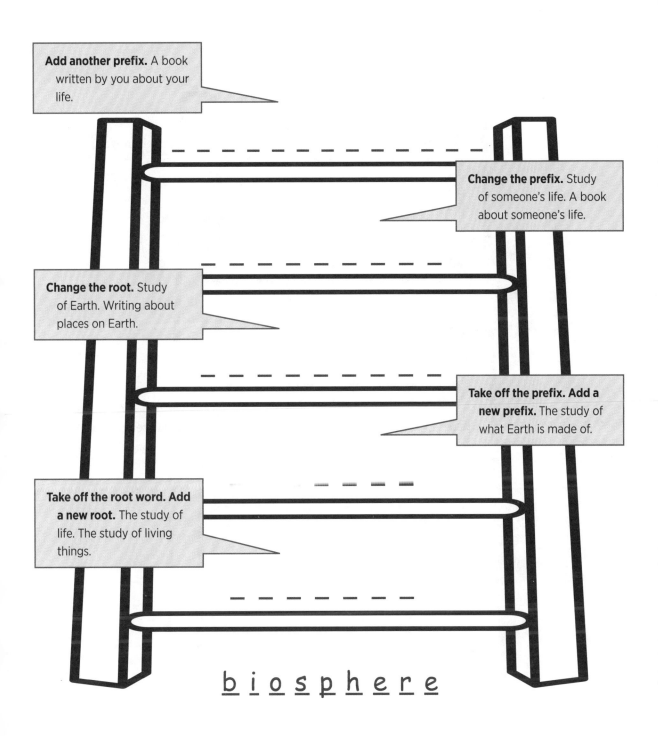

Add another prefix. A book written by you about your life.

Change the prefix. Study of someone's life. A book about someone's life.

Change the root. Study of Earth. Writing about places on Earth.

Take off the prefix. Add a new prefix. The study of what Earth is made of.

Take off the root word. Add a new root. The study of life. The study of living things.

b i o s p h e r e

Lesson Set 21

The Dejected Unicorn

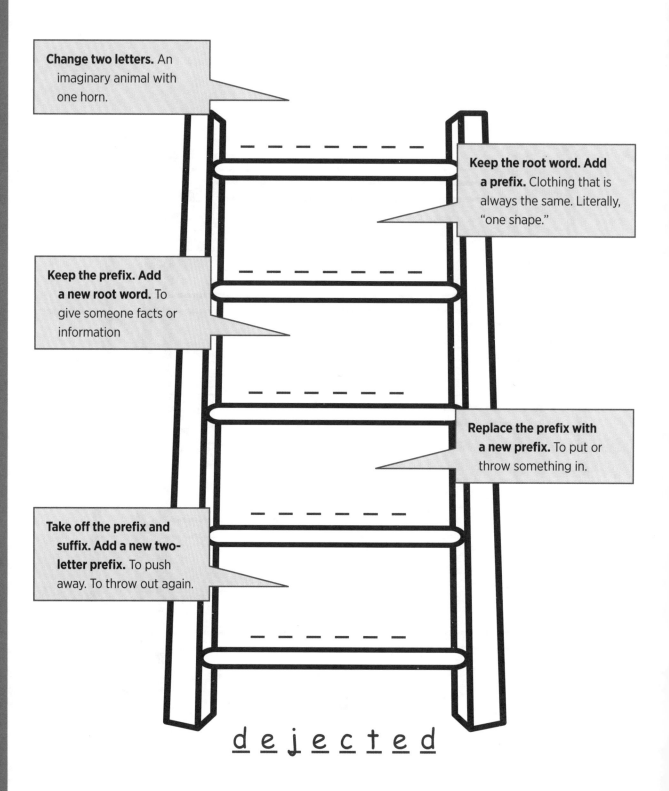

Change two letters. An imaginary animal with one horn.

Keep the root word. Add a prefix. Clothing that is always the same. Literally, "one shape."

Keep the prefix. Add a new root word. To give someone facts or information

Replace the prefix with a new prefix. To put or throw something in.

Take off the prefix and suffix. Add a new two-letter prefix. To push away. To throw out again.

d e j e c t e d

Scope and Sequences

If you don't have a scope and sequence for your spelling instruction, consider one of the following as a starting point. They range from less detailed to more detailed, so pick the one that works best for you.

These scope and sequences are based on a general survey of the current research and various spelling programs, as well as my teaching experiences. They are not grade-level specific. There are two reasons for this. First, it is beyond the scope of this book (no pun intended) to offer a complete instructional scope and sequence for each grade. Second, students who come to you at the beginning of the year may not have mastery over spelling features typically taught in earlier grades. For example, students who have not mastered the basic vowel-team patterns listed in many first- or second-grade scope and sequences may show up in a third-grade classroom. If this classroom is yours, you will have to teach the children what they don't know.

There are two excellent ways to determine which spelling features students know and which they don't. First, analyze the correct spellings and spelling errors of their writing samples. Make sure you pick samples that were written without the help of any teacher or peer. Second, give a spelling inventory at the beginning of the year. Where do you get one to give? Inventories are part of most common spelling programs and usually embedded in core-reading programs as well, so you can often find what you need by looking through those assessment packages. You can also find spelling inventories at my website, www.MarkWeaklandLiteracy.com. Click on the File Cabinet tab at the top of the home page (then look in the left-hand column of the new page). Other inventories can be found with a simple Internet search.

Here's one last thing to consider: Spelling inventories can act as the starting point for a classroom or grade-level spelling scope and sequence. If you don't have a scope and sequence and don't care to use one of the three presented here, consider a spelling inventory as a place to begin constructing one.

General Spelling and Phonics Scope and Sequence, Grades K–6

Feature/Concept	K	1	2	3	4	5	6
Short vowels	*	*					
Consonants	*	*					
Short vowel words (VC, CVC, CVCC)	*	*					
Vowel-consonant-*e* (VCe)		*					
Open-syllable vowels		*					
Blends		*					
Digraphs		*	*				
Vowel teams (monothongs, e.g., *ee*, *ay*)		*	*				
Vowel teams (diphthongs, e.g., *oi*, *ou*)			*				
Schwa in unstressed syllables			*	*	*		
R-controlled vowels			*	*			
Compound words		*	*	*			
Multisyllabic words			*	*	*	*	
Inflectional endings			*	*	*		
Prefixes				*	*	*	
Suffixes				*	*	*	
Greek words and roots						*	*
Latin words and roots						*	*

Syllable Type Scope and Sequence, Grades 1–5

Feature/Concept	K	1	2	3	4	5
Closed syllable	*	*				
Open syllable	*	*				
Vowel-consonant-e syllable (VCe)	*	*				
Open syllable in multisyllabic words			*	*		
Vowel-team syllable		*	*			
Schwa sound/spelling in unstressed syllables			*	*		
R-controlled syllable		*	*			
Consonant-le syllable (C-le)			*	*		
Stable final syllable (leftovers)				*	*	
Combination of all syllable types in multisyllabic word					*	*

Words in bold denote the basic syllable types: closed, open, vowel-consonant-*e*, vowel team, *r*-controlled, consonant-*le*, and stable final.

Specific Spelling/Phonics Scope and Sequence, Grade Bands K–1, 1–2, 2–3, 4–6

Feature/Concept	For Example	K–1	1–2	2–3	4–6
Beginning consonants		*			
Final consonants		*			
Short vowels	*a, e, i, o, u*	*			
Consonant digraphs	*sh, ch, th, wh, wr*		*	*	
Consonant blends	*sl, bl, dr, fr, sp, spr, str*		*		
Closed-syllable exceptions	*ind, ild, ost*		*		
Vowel-consonant-*e*	*a-e, i-e, o-e, u-e*		*		
VCe with *e*	*ole, ore, ure, are, ire*		*	*	
VCe exceptions	*love, have, give*		*		
Long vowels open syllable	*we, go, hi, cry*		*		
Long vowel patterns	*ea, ee, ai, oa, igh*		*		
Other vowel team patterns	*ew, aw, ow, oo oi, oy*			*	
r-controlled vowels	*ar, or, er (ir, or)*		*	*	
Other consonant sounds	*soft c, soft g, ph*			*	
Low-frequency vowel patterns	*ie, au, eigh, ough*			*	
Open multisyllable	*hero, potato*			*	
Inflectional endings	*ing, es, ed, ies*		*	*	
Consonant-*le*	*eagle, pickle, battle*			*	
Suffixes	*en, er, ar, or, ly*			*	
Suffixes	*ure, ate, ize, tion*			*	*
Suffixes	*ment, ful, ness*			*	*
Prefixes	*mis, un, pre, re*			*	*
Schwa sound/spelling in unstressed syllables	*about, Alaska, president*			*	*
Greek root words and roots	*micro, phon, log*				*
Latin root words and roots	*rupt, ject*				*

Lesson Planning Template

Focus Spelling Convention(s) or Feature(s)	Lesson Date

Important Points to Teach, Review, or Remember

Master List	Pre-Test List	Differentiated Lists

Lesson Planning Template (continued)

Sorting Options	

Look Touch Say Options	

Word Ladder	Words to Dictate
	Sentences to Dictate

REFERENCES

Allal, L. 1997. Learning to Spell in the Classroom. In *Learning to Spell,* ed. C.A. Perfetti, L. Rieben, and M. Fayol. Hillsdale, NJ: Lawrence Erlbaum Associates.

Dunlosky, J., K. A. Rawson, E.J. Marsh, M.J. Nathan, and D.T. Willingham. 2013. "Improving Students' Learning with Effective Learning Techniques: Promising Directions from Cognitive and Educational Psychology." *Psychological Science in the Public Interest* 14 (1): 4–58. doi: 10.1177/1529100612453266.

Ehri, L., and S. McCormick. 2013. "Phases of Word Learning: Implications for Instruction with Delayed and Disabled Readers." In *Theoretical Models and Processes of Reading.* 6th ed. Ed. D.E. Alvermann, J.J. Unrau, and R.B. Ruddell. Newark, DE: International Reading Association.

Graham, S. 1983. "Effective Spelling Instruction." *Elementary School Journal* 83 (5): 560–567.

Lehrer, Tom. 1972. *Silent E.* Electric Company: https://www.youtube.com/watch?v=kftn-X26-lg.

McCandliss, B., J. Wise, and Y. Yoncheva. 2015. "Hemispheric Specialization for Visual Words Is Shaped by Attention to Sub-Lexical Units During Initial Learning." *Brain & Language* 145–146: 23–33.

Rapp, B., and K. Lipka. 2011. "The Literate Brain: The Relationship Between Spelling and Reading." *Journal of Cognitive Neuroscience* 23 (5): 1180–1197. doi:10.1162/jocn.2010.21507.

Seidenberg, M. 2016. *Language at the Speed of Sight: How We Read, Why So Many Can't, and What Can Be Done About It.* New York: Basic Books.